Alberta at 100: Celebrating the Legacy

by John Gilpin

Downtown Calgary

Alberta at 100

Celebrating the Legacy

by John Gilpin

cherbo publishing group, inc.

president	JACK C. CHERBO
executive vice president	ELAINE HOFFMAN
editorial director	CHRISTINA M. BEAUSANG
managing feature editor	MARGARET L. MARTIN
feature editor	ERICA RHEINSCHILD
senior profiles editor	J. KELLEY YOUNGER
profiles editors	BENJAMIN PROST
	LIZA YETENEKIAN SMITH
associate editor	SYLVIA EMRICH-TOMA
proofreaders	ANNA BITONG
	ELIZABETH FENNER
	REBECCA SAUER
profiles writers	LINDA CHASE
	SYLVIA EMRICH-TOMA
	KATHLEEN GILBERT
	KRISTINA SAUERWEIN
art director	PERI A. HOLGUIN
senior designer	THEODORE E. YEAGER
designer	LISA MILLER
profiles designers	NELSON CAMPOS
	THEODORE E. YEAGER
photo editors	WALTER MLADINA
	DAVID ZANZINGER
digital color specialist	ART VASQUEZ
sales administrator	JOAN K. BAKER
profile services supervisor	PATRICIA DE LEONARD
profile services coordinators	KENYA HICKS
	LESLIE E. SHAW
administrative assistants	KELLY PASSALAQUA
	JUDY ROBITSCHEK
	BILL WAY
publisher's representative	BEVERLEY A. CORNELL

Cherbo Publishing Group, Inc.
Encino, California 91316
© 2006 by Cherbo Publishing Group, Inc.
All rights reserved. Published 2006.
Printed by Friesens
Altona, Manitoba, Canada,
and Minneapolis, Minnesota, USA

ISBN 978-1-882933-71-6

Visit the CPG Web site at www.cherbopub.com.

The information in this publication is the most recent available and has been carefully researched to ensure accuracy. Cherbo Publishing Group, Inc. cannot and does not guarantee either the correctness of all information furnished it or the complete absence of errors, including omissions.

Oil drilling platform near Edmonton

ACKNOWLEDGMENTS

The writing of this book was greatly assisted by the staff at the Glenbow Library and Archives, who freely shared their knowledge of the collection and made numerous valuable suggestions as to where the appropriate material could be located. Jonathan Hanna, the corporate historian of the Canadian Pacific Railway, provided valuable information as well.

DEDICATION

To the past, present, and future generations of Albertans.

Fairmont Chateau Lake Louise, Banff National Park

Table of Contents

Edmonton

Calf roundup, Duchess

Companies and Organizations Profiled

The following organizations made a valuable commitment to the quality of this publication. The local chambers of commerce and departments of economic development gratefully acknowledge their participation in *Alberta at 100: Celebrating the Legacy*.

Watermark Tower, Calgary

Business Visionaries

The following companies and organizations are innovators in their fields and have played a prominent role in this publication, as they have in Alberta's communities.

BG Group plc
Thames Valley Park Drive, Reading, Berkshire RG6 1PT UK
Phone: +44-0-118-935-3222
E-mail: Box.info@bg-group.com

BG Canada Exploration and Production, Inc.
Suite 700, 150-Sixth Avenue SW, Calgary, AB T2P 3Y7,
Canada
Phone: 403-538-7400/Fax: 403-538-7500
Web site: www.bg-group.com
A Global Natural Gas Business

BG CANADA

Best Communities.
Best Value. Since 1958.

Carma Developers LP
Calgary (Head Office)
7315-Eighth Street NE, Calgary, AB T2E 8A2, Canada
Phone: 403-231-8900/Fax: 403-231-8960
E-mail: calgaryinfo@carma.ca
Web site: www.carma.ca

Horton CBI, Limited
Highway 825, Sturgeon Industrial Park, Fort Saskatchewan, AB T8L2T4,
Canada
Phone: 780-998-2800/Fax: 780-998-2841
Marc R. Beauregard, President
Contact: Christian R. Desjardins, Business Development Manager
E-mail: cdesjardins@CBI.com
Web site: www.CBI.com

Focused • Competitive • Local
Results Second to None

KINDER MORGAN
CANADA INC.

Kinder Morgan Canada Inc.
Suite 2700, 300-Fifth Avenue SW, Calgary, AB, T2P 5J2, Canada
Phone: 403-514-6400 or 800-535-7219/Fax: 403-514-6459
Contact: Tracey Goldberg, Graphic Production Coordinator
E-mail: info@kindermorgan.com
Web site: www.kindermorgan.com
A Different Kind of Energy Company

Prudential Steel Ltd.
1800, 140-Fourth Avenue SW, Calgary, AB T2P 3N3, Canada
Phone: 403-267-0300 or 800-661-1050/Fax: 403-265-3426
Contact: Guy Cocquyt, Director Business Development
E-mail: info@prudentialsteel.com
Web site: www.prudentialsteel.com
Partners in Quality

PRUDENTIAL STEEL LTD.
Partners In Quality

Walton International Group Inc.
HEADQUARTERS
605-Fifth Avenue SW, 23rd Floor,
Calgary, AB T2P 3H5, Canada
Phone: 403-265-4255/Fax: 403-261-2503
Contact: Bill Doherty, President and CEO
E-mail: info@waltoninternational.com
Web site: www.waltoninternational.com
Investing on Solid Ground

Additional locations:
CANADA
Edmonton, AB; Vancouver, BC; Saskatoon, SK;
Toronto and Ottawa, ON

ASIA
Hong Kong; Singapore; Kuala Lumpur, Malaysia;
Hangzhou, China; Jakarta, Indonesia

UNITED STATES
Phoenix, Arizona

Walton
International Group Inc.

Foreword

Alberta's second century has begun. As we move forward, it is important that we reflect on our roots. *Alberta at 100: Celebrating the Legacy* gives readers an opportunity to look back at the industries, events, and people that helped make Alberta the province it is today.

Like many projects created to mark Alberta's 100th anniversary milestone, this book highlights Alberta's strengths and achievements. The past century has been a time of tremendous growth for our province. Albertans have done well to capitalize on these changing times. Thanks to the ingenuity, determination, and spirit of those who built our province, we are ready for the future. Our legacy is a province of unlimited promise.

As the province's centennial passes into memory, I am pleased that books like *Alberta at 100: Celebrating the Legacy* will continue to celebrate the wonderful place we are proud to call home.

Gary G. Mar, Q.C

Minister of Community Development
M.L.A. Calgary Mackay

Light Rail Transit Line, 7th Avenue, Calgary

Historical Highlights

Alberta's rugged frontier beckoned the adventurous, who tapped its potential and transformed it into a centre of commerce and culture. That pioneering spirit remains in Alberta, where scientific discoveries, economic boons, and creative endeavors are a way of life.

1670	1778	1795	1861	1870

1670—King Charles II of Great Britain gives the Hudson's Bay Company the territory of Rupert's Land, which consists of what is presently Ontario, Manitoba, northern Quebec, most of Saskatchewan, southern and central Alberta, and portions of the Northwest Territories and Nunavut.

1778—Alberta's first fur-trading post is set up near the delta of the Athabasca River, south of Lake Athabasca, by Peter Pond, who would later help establish the North West Company.

1861—With help from the Métis, Father Albert Lacombe builds the St. Albert Roman Catholic Mission near Fort Edmonton, which becomes the centre of a French-speaking settlement. Today its restored chapel is Alberta's oldest building.

1870—The Hudson's Bay Company sells Rupert's Land to the new confederation of Canada for 300,000 pounds sterling ($1,460,000 Canadian), and the vast area is officially named the North-West Territories.

1754–55—The Hudson's Bay Company sends Anthony Henday inland to convince First Nations people to come to the company's York Factory on Hudson Bay to trade. Henday's report on his travels is the first recorded visit of central Alberta.

1795—The North West Company builds Fort Augustus at the confluence of the Sturgeon and North Saskatchewan rivers, near modern-day Fort Saskatchewan. That year, the Hudson's Bay Company builds its own post, Fort Edmonton, at the same location. Fort Edmonton will be moved to present-day Edmonton in 1830 and become one of the largest and most important fur-trading centres in Alberta.

First Nations peoples

Father Albert Lacombe, circa 1886–1894

Banff Springs Hotel, Banff National Park, circa late 1880s

1874	1882	1883	1884	1892

1884—As geologist Joseph Burr Tyrrell is exploring along the Red Deer River in what is presently Drumheller, he discovers the skull and skeleton of a dinosaur which is later named "Albertosaurus." A cousin of *Tyrannosaurus rex*, the dinosaur is the first of its kind to be found.

1874—Fort Macleod, the first North-West Mounted Police post in Alberta, is created to suppress the whiskey trade and to establish Canadian control of the expansive North-West Territories. Another post, Fort Calgary, will follow in 1875.

1882—The North-West Territories is divided into four provisional districts: Alberta, Assiniboia, Athabaska, and Saskatchewan.

1883—While constructing the Canadian Pacific Railway (CPR) near Sulphur Mountain, workers discover hot springs, leading to the creation of Banff National Park, Canada's first national park.

1892—Edmonton, which has about 700 residents, is incorporated as a town. It will be named the province's capital in 1906.

1875—The Canadian Parliament adopts the North-West Territories Act to establish permanent institutions of government for the territories.

1882—African-American John Ware helps bring a herd of cattle to Alberta, as part of a cattle drive from Montana, and settles in the Calgary area. Ware's outstanding equestrian abilities will make him a ranching legend.

1883—The CPR completes a main line from Walsh, near the Saskatchewan border, west to Lake Louise, near the British Columbia border. The railway will become a catalyst for settlement and economic development in Alberta.

1892—A group of 23 Ukrainian families settles in east central Alberta. By 1931, Alberta's Ukrainian population will have grown to more than 55,000. Buildings originally located in the communities established by these immigrants will eventually be moved to create the Ukrainian Cultural Heritage Village, east of Edmonton.

John Ware at Red Deer River, 1901

Historical Highlights

1894	1903	1905	1909	1912
1894—Calgary, with a population of 4,000, is incorporated as a city.	1903—Dr. William Fairfield, director of the Lethbridge Model Farm, discovers how to grow alfalfa in Alberta. Following Dr. Fairfield's discovery, alfalfa becomes a key crop for Canada's burgeoning livestock industry.	1905—Alberta, named for Princess Louise Caroline Alberta, becomes a province of Canada.	1909—Calgary's first sky-scraper, the six-storey Calgary Grain Exchange Building, is constructed. It is one of the tallest buildings in Alberta at the time.	1912—Financed by the City of Calgary and American industrialist Andrew Carnegie, Alberta's first library opens in Calgary's Central Park and becomes the city's cultural centre.
	1903—In less than two minutes, 82 million metric tons of limestone rock slide down Turtle Mountain and bury a section of Frank, a coal mining town in the Crowsnest Pass; 70 people are killed. The Frank Slide Interpretive Centre will be established 82 years later to commemorate this historical event.	1906—The University of Alberta is founded in Edmonton. The university will become one of Alberta's largest research institutions and hold the record for 3M Teaching Fellowships, Canada's top award for under-graduate teaching excellence.		

Science and Arts Building,
University of Alberta, 1912

Prince of Wales Ranch, 1927

1914	1916	1919	1927	1929
			1927—The "Famous Five," Albertans Henrietta Muir Edwards, Louise McKinney, Nellie McLung, Emily Murphy, and Irene Parlby, challenge the ruling that the word "persons" in the British North America Act excludes women from the Senate. They will lose their case in the Supreme Court.	1929—The Famous Five battle again to be included in the Senate and this time win the right from the Judicial Committee of the Privy Council of Great Britain, the highest Court of Appeal in Canada at the time.
1914—The Dingman #1 well near Turner Valley strikes natural gas and naphtha, heralding a new industrial era in Alberta, one based on energy.	1916—Prohibition is enacted in Alberta; it will last eight years.	1919—Edward, Prince of Wales (later King Edward VIII), is the first royal to make an official visit to Alberta. He is so taken with the province's ranch country that he purchases a 4,000-acre ranch near Calgary.		
1914—Unexplained explosions tear through the Hillcrest Mine in the Crowsnest Pass, killing 189 men in Canada's worst mine disaster.	1916—Alberta, Manitoba, and Saskatchewan are the first Canadian provinces to grant women the right to vote in provincial elections.	1923—The first Calgary Exhibition and Stampede takes place. The event is formed when the Calgary Exhibition, an agricultural show which began in 1886, joins with the Calgary Stampede, a cowboy rodeo which debuted in 1912. The annual event will become a world-famous attraction, drawing millions of visitors.		

Historical Highlights

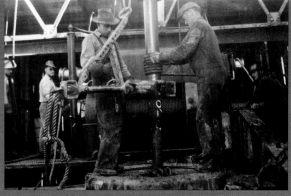

Drilling of Imperial Oil's Leduc #1 Well, 1947

1930

1930—The Alberta Natural Resources Act transfers control of the province's natural resources from the federal government to Alberta's government, resulting in greater economic security and prosperity for the province.

1933—The Banff Centre is founded by the University of Alberta Department of Extension and begins with one drama class. It will become a globally respected arts, cultural, and educational facility.

1936

Charles Noble (right), Nobleford, date unknown

1936—Alberta farmer Charles Sherwood Noble invents the Noble Blade, designed to leave the topmost layer of dirt intact while cutting through weeds and stubble. His invention will help save agriculture in Alberta's arid southern prairies.

1938

1938—The Métis Population Betterment Act is enacted by the Alberta government to set aside 12 lands for settlement. The act also includes hunting and trapping rights and a framework for establishing associations which have authority to manage the settlements.

1946—A Calgary branch of the University of Alberta is founded. In 1966, it will become a separate university, the University of Calgary, and eventually blossom into one of Canada's top research universities, with more than 30 research institutes and centres on campus.

1947

1947—Oil is struck at Leduc, leading to the discovery of Canada's core oil reserves and triggering an oil boom that makes Alberta's the largest and most prosperous prairie economy.

1948

Calgary Stampeders' 1948 Grey Cup celebration

1948—The Calgary Stampeders win their first Grey Cup in a 12–7 win against the Ottawa Rough Riders, the culmination of the footballers' perfect 12–0 season. The Stampeders will go on to win four more Grey Cups.

1948—The Edmonton Eskimo football team is established. The team will become one of the most successful in Canadian football history, winning 11 Grey Cups.

1957	1958	1961	1966	1967

1957—Writing-On-Stone Provincial Park near Milk River is created. Twenty years later, a portion of the park will become an archaeological preserve to protect North America's largest concentration of rock art created by Plains people.

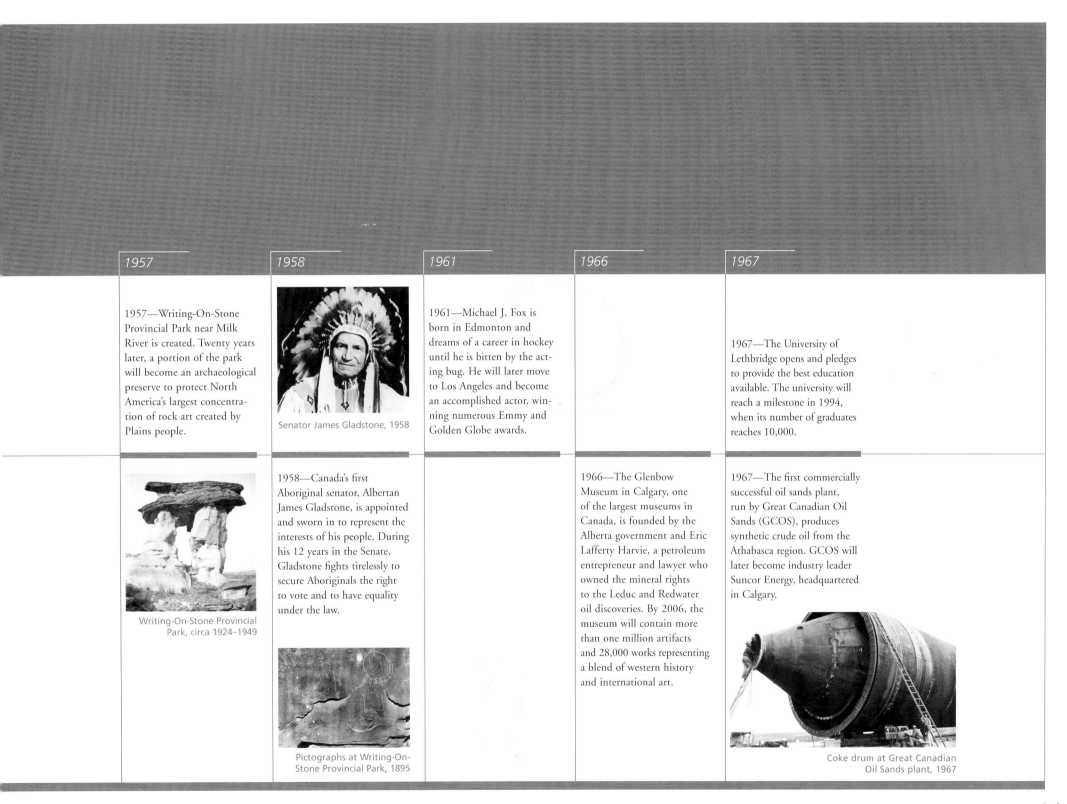

Senator James Gladstone, 1958

1961—Michael J. Fox is born in Edmonton and dreams of a career in hockey until he is bitten by the acting bug. He will later move to Los Angeles and become an accomplished actor, winning numerous Emmy and Golden Globe awards.

1967—The University of Lethbridge opens and pledges to provide the best education available. The university will reach a milestone in 1994, when its number of graduates reaches 10,000.

Writing-On-Stone Provincial Park, circa 1924–1949

1958—Canada's first Aboriginal senator, Albertan James Gladstone, is appointed and sworn in to represent the interests of his people. During his 12 years in the Senate, Gladstone fights tirelessly to secure Aboriginals the right to vote and to have equality under the law.

Pictographs at Writing-On-Stone Provincial Park, 1895

1966—The Glenbow Museum in Calgary, one of the largest museums in Canada, is founded by the Alberta government and Eric Lafferty Harvie, a petroleum entrepreneur and lawyer who owned the mineral rights to the Leduc and Redwater oil discoveries. By 2006, the museum will contain more than one million artifacts and 28,000 works representing a blend of western history and international art.

1967—The first commercially successful oil sands plant, run by Great Canadian Oil Sands (GCOS), produces synthetic crude oil from the Athabasca region. GCOS will later become industry leader Suncor Energy, headquartered in Calgary.

Coke drum at Great Canadian Oil Sands plant, 1967

Historical Highlights

| 1968 | 1970 | 1981 | 1983 | 1984 |

1968—Alberta adopts a flag that features a coat of arms shield on a royal blue background. The shield symbolizes the province's British heritage and varied topography.

1970—Athabasca University, now Canada's leading distance-education and online university, is founded.

1974—Alberta's first Aboriginal lieutenant-governor, Ralph Garvin Steinhauer, is appointed.

1981—Head-Smashed-In Buffalo Jump, the oldest, largest, and best-preserved buffalo jump site known to exist in the world, is designated a UNESCO World Heritage Site.

Alberta's flag

1979—Dinosaur Provincial Park, located in the heart of Alberta's badlands, is declared a UNESCO World Heritage Site. Established in 1955, the park is world-renowned for its dinosaur fossil beds which have yielded bones from 35 dinosaur species.

1981—The first phase of the world's largest enclosed shopping mall, West Edmonton Mall, is completed. Phases two, three, and four will be completed in 1983, 1985, and 1998, respectively. Developed by Edmonton-based Triple Five Group, the mall will ultimately total 5.2 million square feet and include 800 stores, 110 restaurants, a 360-room hotel, and a full-scale amusement park.

1983—The Edmonton Space Sciences Centre, designed by award-winning Aboriginal architect and Calgary native Douglas J. Cardinal, is completed. The centre is a blend of art and science which represents a place where the landscape meets the vastness and fantasy of space.

1984—The Edmonton Oilers win their first Stanley Cup Championship with help from Wayne Gretzky, "The Great One." The team will win four more championships, in 1985, 1987, 1988, and 1990.

1986—Dr. Lorne Tyrell, a professor at the University of Alberta, begins investigating a cure for hepatitis B. His work will lead to the development of the first oral medicine for the virus.

Wayne Gretzky with Stanley Cup trophy, 1984

ISU World Figure Skating Championships 2006

1988

1988—The XV Olympic Winter Games deliver multimillion-dollar profits to Calgary and feature a number of Olympic firsts, including indoor speed skating, alpine events on artificial snow, and an expanded 16 days of competition.

1988—Alberta native and four-time World Figure Skating Champion Kurt Browning skates his way into the *Guinness Book of Records* as he performs the first quadruple jump ever completed in a competition, at the World Championships in Budapest, Hungary.

1988 Olympics venue Pengrowth Saddledome

1989

1989—The Calgary Flames beat the Montreal Canadiens to win their first Stanley Cup. The year also marks the first time Soviet hockey players are allowed to sign with NHL teams.

1991—Calgary native James Gosling invents the programming language Java while employed by U.S.–based Sun Microsystems.

2001

2001—The National Institute for Nanotechnology is established in Edmonton to conduct revolutionary research at the atomic scale.

2004

2004—Between 1994 and 2004 Alberta's exports of goods and services more than double, reaching $73.2 billion, and Alberta's investment per capita doubles to $15,157—twice the national average.

2005—Alberta marks its 100th birthday with simultaneous celebrations in 10 communities and a royal visit from Queen Elizabeth II.

2006

2006—Alberta is the first Canadian province featured at the Smithsonian Folklife Festival, an annual event celebrating cultural heritage, in Washington, D.C.

2006—The ISU World Figure Skating Championships 2006 are held at Pengrowth Saddledome in Calgary.

2006—Stephen Harper is sworn in as Canada's 22nd prime minister. A University of Calgary graduate, Harper was first elected to the House of Commons in 1993 as the Reform Party's candidate in Calgary West.

Part One

Business Minded
Alberta Industry Then and Now

Chapter One
Transportation and Tourism

On the Go

For more than two centuries, transportation has played a key role in Alberta life, facilitating the province's settlement and spurring its economic development. Much has changed since the late 1700s, when Alberta's rivers were the region's primary transportation and trading routes. Today Alberta boasts a complex network of railways, highways, and airports which have the capacity to make local resources and products accessible to the world.

Several industries owe their existence to the development of this system, including Alberta's tourism sector, which was launched by the arrival of the Canadian Pacific Railway (CPR) in 1883. As an efficient system of highways and airports evolved in the 20th century, tourism quickly became one of the fastest-growing sectors of the economy. Tourism is now a leading industry in Alberta, with receipts of about $4.6 billion in 2004.

HPPGOOD BROS. CAMP
GPR 1907

Previous spread: An airplane lands at Calgary International Airport. This page, above: Canadian Pacific Railway (CPR) labourers set up a construction camp near Hughenden in 1907. This page, right: Steam billows from a 110-tonne CPR locomotive, circa late 1800s. Opposite page: A CPR train carrying potash travels through Alberta en route to Vancouver.

Wheels of Progress

Alberta's northern rivers formed the basis of the region's earliest transportation system. Used by First Nations, these rivers became important passageways for fur traders in the late 18th century. Life and commerce in Alberta was forever changed in 1883, when the CPR completed a rail main line from Walsh, near the Saskatchewan border, west to Lake Louise, near the British Columbia border. By 1898, the Montreal-based company had developed a branch line network extending north to Edmonton, south to Coutts, and west via the Crowsnest Pass to British Columbia.

Attracting settlers to the west was an immediate priority for the CPR, since it needed to create a demand for its freight and passenger services. To entice people into the area, the company distributed pamphlets extolling the virtues of the west and exhibited agricultural products grown in the region. The CPR's efforts helped create a land boom which lasted from 1896 to 1913.

During the early years of the railroad, the CPR created an entirely new economy and settlement pattern in what was once a sparsely populated region. By 1890, 64 towns had formed along the CPR's railways in Alberta.

One of the most dramatically affected towns was Calgary, which

had begun as a North-West Mounted Police post on the Bow River. Once the CPR main line was completed nearby in 1883, the town moved three-quarters of a mile west to be nearer the railway. Soon thereafter, Calgary civic leaders convinced the CPR to establish stockyards in the city, and in 1911, the company chose Calgary for its main western repair facility, Ogden Shops. In a matter of just a few years, the CPR had become Calgary's largest employer.

While the CPR was developing networks in southern Alberta, a number of other railroad companies were focusing on the northern part of the province. By 1915, Edmonton had been incorporated into Canada's transcontinental railway system. The construction of railways northwest and northeast from Edmonton between 1907 and 1924 enhanced the city's role as the gateway to the north.

The expansion of the Alberta railway system came to an end in 1930, when the Depression drastically reduced the need for transportation services. Unemployed men riding in freight trains became an enduring image of the era. The commencement of World War II, however, provided railway companies an opportunity to operate at full capacity again. Large numbers of soldiers, military equipment, and war materials were transported via rail during this time. Alberta's railways returned to carrying

passengers and freight after the war, and the economic momentum the war generated continued.

Alberta's transportation sector got another boost in 1996, when the CPR moved its headquarters from Montreal to Calgary. Today the CPR's headquarters is also home to the company's Network Management Center, where train movements throughout Canada are orchestrated and controlled. The CPR, whose 22,500-kilometre network extends from Montreal to Vancouver and to the United States, has additional facilities in Edmonton, Lethbridge, Medicine Hat, and Red Deer.

This page, left: A quiet moment is captured at Ogden Shops in 1912. Opposite page: The CPR's routes through Canada are illustrated in this 1882 poster.

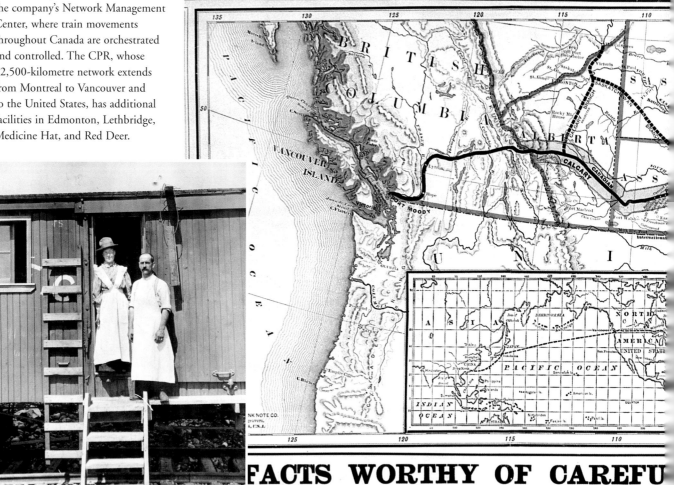

THE CANA

VERSING THE GREAT

To the Rich Grazing Grounds and Cattle Ranches at the Eastern Bas

FACTS WORTHY OF CAREFU

DIAN PACIFIC RAILWAY.
WHEAT REGION OF THE CANADIAN NORTHW

the Rocky Mountains.   Total Length Main Line, 2,760 Miles.   The Richest Soil, the Healthiest Climate, and the Cheapest Farming Land in the World.

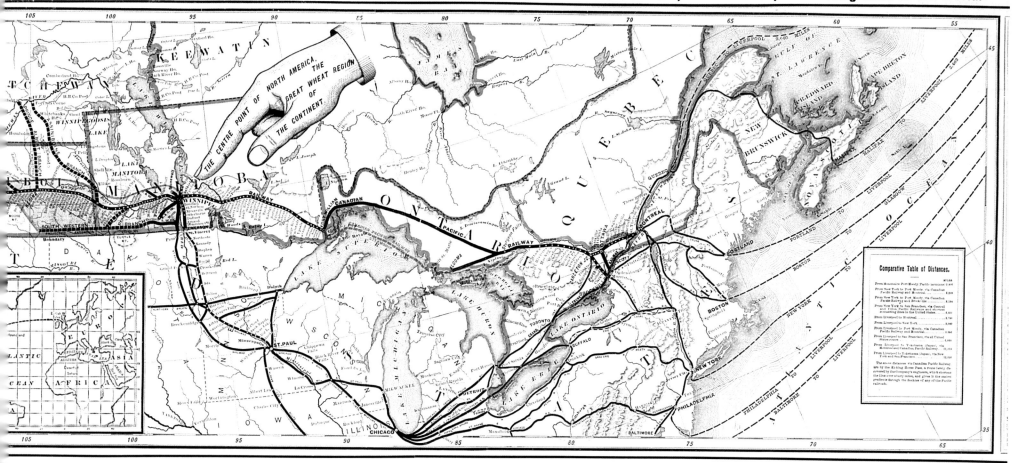

READING ABOUT MANITOBA and THE GREAT CANADIAN NORTHW

Trails to Highways

Long before paved highways criss-crossed Alberta, trails and dirt roads provided vital links between towns. Rugged and sometimes dangerous, these routes were a major challenge for travellers, especially after it rained. Difficult as they were to use, they remained a feature of the Alberta road system in some locations until the 1950s.

In the 1920s and 1930s, the Alberta government began gravelling and paving dirt roads. One of the largest projects of the period was the Mackenzie Highway, the first road to link Alberta with the Northwest Territories. Connecting Grimshaw with Wrigley, the 548-kilometre highway was started in 1937 and took 12 years to complete.

Between 1950 and 1955, the portion of the Trans-Canada Highway in Alberta was paved from the Saskatchewan border to Calgary. In 1955, the first four-lane divided highway in the province—Highway 2 between Calgary and Airdrie—was constructed. Additional highway projects followed, including the Alberta portion of the Yellowhead Highway, stretching from Lloydminster at the Saskatchewan border to Jasper near the British Columbia border, which was completed in 1970.

More recently, the Alberta government began developing a four-lane divided highway from Calgary to Coutts on the Montana border, and from Edmonton northwest to the British Columbia border. To be completed by 2007, the highway is part of the CANAMEX corridor, a cooperative effort by Canada, the United States, and Mexico to provide a transportation link from Alaska to Mexico.

Improved highways and access to national and international markets have made Alberta a strategic location for commercial trucking companies, some of which have become industry leaders. One such company is Trimac Group, whose roots go back to 1945. The Calgary-based firm is now one of the largest transporters of bulk commodities in North America. Mullen Group, in Aldersyde, is another top commercial trucking company in Alberta. Founded in 1949, the company is western Canada's leading provider of specialized transportation for the oil and gas industry.

This page: A building crew works on the Trans-Canada Highway in Alberta in 1957. Opposite page: Trucks travel along the Trans-Canada Highway, near the Alberta-Saskatchewan border.

This page: Alberta's first official prairie mail service flight prepares for takeoff in Edmonton in 1930. Opposite page: An Air Canada plane leaves Edmonton International Airport.

Wings over Alberta

At the beginning of the 20th century, a new form of transportation—aviation—was taking off, and Albertans were quick to embrace it. The first flight in Alberta took place in 1909, when Reginald Hunt flew for 35 minutes over the rooftops of Edmonton at altitudes of 35 to 50 feet in a plane he designed himself. In 1926, the City of Edmonton built Canada's first municipally licensed airport. This airport, which became known as the Municipal, was the base of operations for bush pilots as well as for air mail flights and military operations during World War II. Now known as Edmonton City Centre Airport, the facility is used for corporate and general aviation purposes.

Edmonton expanded its airport facilities in the 1960s, opening the Edmonton International Airport (EIA) in 1963. Originally designed to accommodate 2.5 million passengers, the airport surpassed this figure by 1981. Currently Canada's fifth-busiest airport, EIA handled a record 4.5 million passengers in 2005.

In 1928, Calgary followed Edmonton's example and purchased land to develop civic airports. In 1939, the city built McCall Field, which was named after Captain Fred McCall, one of Calgary's aviation pioneers. Just a year after the airport opened, however, it was taken over by the federal government to serve the war effort. During this time, McCall Field was used to train pilots and to deliver planes to the Soviet Union. Following the war, normal operations resumed and the airport gradually expanded to meet the needs of the growing aviation industry. By the 1960s, McCall Field was commonly called Calgary International Airport. Today Calgary International is the country's fourth-busiest airport, serving more than 10 million people in 2005, an all-time high.

Alberta's two international airports are supported by regional airports in Lethbridge, Medicine Hat, Red Deer, Fort McMurray, Grande Prairie, and Peace River. This well-developed network of airports has been key to local airline companies such as Kenn Borek Air and WestJet Airlines. Headquartered in Calgary and established in 1970, Kenn Borek provides air support for United Nations peacekeeping missions, North and South Pole scientific teams, and oil drilling operations. Calgary-based WestJet, which began service in 1996, flies to more than 30 destinations in North America.

This page, left: A colorful poster beckons vacationers to Banff National Park in 1930. This page, right: Fresh powder lures skiers to Banff's slopes. Opposite page: The Canadian Rockies create an exquisite backdrop for the Prince of Wales Hotel in Waterton Lakes National Park.

Rocky Mountain Tourism

During the CPR main line's construction in 1883, a cave with hot springs was discovered at the foot of Sulphur Mountain. This gave the CPR's general manager, William Cornelius Van Horne, a brilliant idea. "Since we can't export the scenery," he said, "we shall have to import the tourists." Van Horne worked with government officials to designate the area surrounding the springs and the town site of Banff as Canada's first national park. His plan to develop Banff as a tourist destination included obtaining first-class passenger coaches and constructing the grand Banff Springs Hotel, which opened in 1888. Van Horne also hired Swiss mountain guides to take hotel guests up to the highest nearby peaks. Banff National Park's majestic beauty captured the imaginations of

wealthy travellers, and thus Alberta's tourism industry was born.

Waterton Lakes National Park to the south of Banff and Jasper National Park to the north were established next. Designated a national park in 1911, Waterton Lakes National Park began as a forest reserve which was used as a camping and picnic resort by residents of nearby settlements. As the park grew in popularity, tourist facilities were constructed, including the stately Prince of Wales hotel in 1927. In 1932, the Canadian and U.S. governments proclaimed Waterton Lakes National Park and Glacier National Park in Montana the Waterton–Glacier International Peace Park. Chief Mountain International Highway, built in

This page: Conventioneers make their way to an event at the Shaw Convention Centre in Edmonton. Opposite page, left: The fearsome jaws of a velociraptor do nothing to intimidate a young visitor at the Royal Tyrrell Museum in Drumheller. Opposite page, right: Chuck wagon racing thrills crowds at the world-famous Calgary Stampede.

1935, provided a direct link between the two parks.

Jasper National Park was established in 1907 as a pathway for Canada's second transcontinental railway, the Grand Trunk Pacific Railway. During the next 20 years, various changes were made to the park's boundaries, eventually making it Canada's largest national park.

By the late 1930s, highways connecting Banff, Jasper, and Waterton to Alberta's urban centres had expanded access to the parks. Today Alberta's national parks draw more than six million people each year.

A Provincial Industry

Tourist attractions were created beyond the mountain parks as well. In 1917, two mule deer were captured in Calgary and put on display at St. George's Island. The display was the precursor to the Calgary Zoo, which officially opened in 1929. The Calgary Zoo now has more than 1,000 animals and hosts more than one million visitors annually.

The Alberta tourism industry expanded further when the Provincial Museum of Alberta, known today as the Royal Alberta Museum, opened in Edmonton in 1967. More cultural sites followed in the 1980s, including Head-Smashed-In Buffalo Jump near Fort Macleod, which was designated as a UNESCO World Heritage Site in 1981; the Odyssium science museum in Edmonton in 1984; and the acclaimed Royal Tyrrell Museum of paleontology in Drumheller in 1985.

These attractions are now among the most-visited in the province.

World-class sporting events add yet another dimension to the Alberta tourism industry. In 1988, Calgary hosted the XV Olympic Winter Games, which pumped an extra $158 million into Calgary's economy. Calgary is also home to one of the largest rodeo events in the world, the Calgary Stampede. The event got its start in 1886 and now attracts more than one million people annually.

The Calgary Stampede was the inspiration for Canada's first publicly owned convention centre, the Telus Convention Centre. First suggested as part of a Stampede expansion plan in 1962, the centre opened in Calgary in 1974. Eleven years later, the Shaw Convention Centre was completed in Edmonton. Seventy percent underground, the centre was built into the bank of the valley of the North Saskatchewan River. Today these convention centres, along with some 1,100 hotels, support the province's multifaceted tourism industry.

Alberta's railways, highways, and airports link the province to the world, while its tourism sector welcomes visitors from near and far. Together, these industries fuel economic growth, securing Alberta's role as a land of opportunity.

Field and Forest Wealth

Alberta's rolling foothills and fertile soil held great promise for ranchers and settlers in the 1800s. The livestock these pioneers raised and the land they tilled gave rise to agriculture and food processing industries which remain a vital part of the province's economy. Today Alberta is Canada's second-largest agri-food exporter and its third-largest food and beverage producer.

Another abundant resource, trees, played a pivotal role in Alberta's development as well. Used for constructing railroads and new towns in the late 1800s, Alberta's trees now fuel a forestry industry which produces everything from paper to furniture and which generated $3.4 billion in exports in 2004.

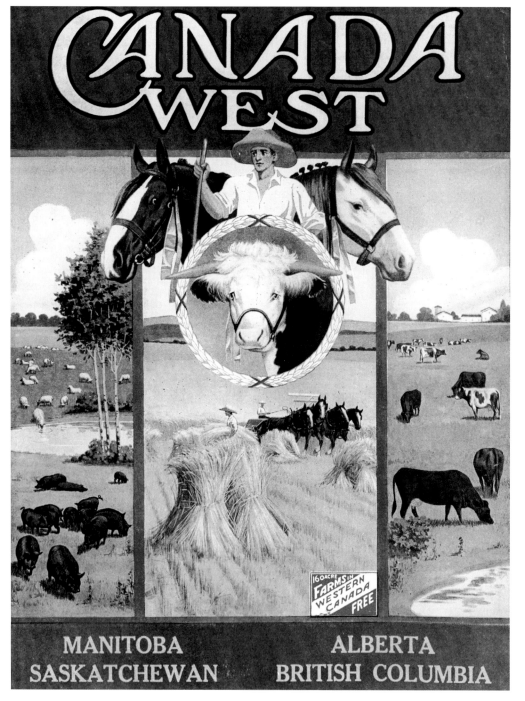

CANADA WEST

MANITOBA
SASKATCHEWAN

ALBERTA
BRITISH COLUMBIA

160 ACRE FARMS IN WESTERN CANADA FREE

Alberta Is Beef Country

In 1873, Methodist missionary John McDougall brought a herd of breeding cattle to his father's new mission at Morleyville on the Bow River. The cattle, which ultimately financed the mission, were the first to arrive in southern Alberta. Eight years after McDougall and his cattle arrived in Alberta, the Canadian government introduced a policy permitting ranching companies to lease up to 100,000 acres at one cent an acre in the west. Large ranching operations were quickly established in Alberta, and stock for these new ranches was brought in from Montana. The influx of settlers, however, prompted the federal government to cancel all large leases in 1896, allowing the land to be broken up for settlement. This policy change, combined with the severe winter of 1906–1907, took a heavy toll on cattle herds and put the ranching industry into a steep decline. To give cattlemen a secure land base to develop the industry, the federal government introduced 21-year closed leases of the land in 1925.

One of the large ranches which successfully adapted to the various changes in the industry was the Bar U Ranch. Established in Longview in 1881, the ranch had become a centre of breeding excellence by the 1920s. It was one of the country's leading ranches until the 1950s and became a National Historic Site in 1991.

As Alberta's ranches were being established, so, too, were meatpacking businesses. Initially a small industry, meat processing grew rapidly after railways were constructed in the 1880s. One of the first people to establish a successful meatpacking company in Alberta was Patrick Burns, who built a small slaughterhouse in east Calgary in the 1890s. The business he founded, which survived until 1996, became a model for other meatpackers.

The 1960s were a time of tremendous growth for meat processing in Alberta, and by 1965, Alberta had become Canada's largest beef producer. More expansion followed in the 1980s with the arrival of Cargill Foods, which built Canada's largest fully integrated beef processing facility in High River.

Although Alberta's meat processing industry seemed unstoppable, it

suffered a serious setback in 2003, when a cow with bovine spongiform encephalopathy (BSE), commonly referred to as mad cow disease, was discovered on a farm near Wanham. As a result, the United States, Japan, South Korea, Australia, and Mexico closed their borders to Canadian beef and live cattle exports. Canada immediately reviewed its animal testing program and began promoting domestic consumption of beef to offset the loss of export revenue.

The United States reopened its borders to some Canadian beef in late 2003, and imports of young Canadian cattle resumed in 2005.

Despite the BSE crisis, Alberta continues to be Canada's largest cattle-producing province. Cattle and calf inventories were 5.9 million in 2005, representing more than a third of the national total. Contributing to the industry's success are companies such as Cargill Foods, Lakeside Packers,

and XL Foods. The province's largest meat processor, Cargill Foods processes 4,000 head of cattle daily at its High River facility. The company is a subsidiary of Excel Corporation in Kansas. Lakeside, headquartered in Brooks and Alberta's second-largest meatpacking company, began operations in 1966. Today it is a subsidiary of Arkansas-based Tyson Foods. XL Foods, based in Edmonton, processes more than 450,000 head of cattle each year. Founded in 1971 and

owned by Nilsson Brothers in Edmonton, XL has plants in Calgary and Edmonton. Nilsson also operates Canada's largest cattle auction market in Clyde.

Cultivating an Industry

Alberta's agriculture industry had an inauspicious start. When John Palliser traveled to southern Alberta in 1858 as part of a British exploration of the North-West Territories, he described the barren region as an

Previous spread: The sun sets on a farmer taking stock of his crop in Three Hills. This page, left: Cattle graze on a hill in southern Alberta. This page, right: Meatpacking pioneer Patrick Burns is seen in a photograph from 1927. Opposite page: A pamphlet advertising free farms in western Canada promises bountiful harvests.

extension of the Great American Desert. Dry conditions in the late 1850s had certainly influenced Palliser's pessimistic view, but by the 1870s, rain had rejuvenated the soil. In the next 10 years, the Canadian Pacific Railway (CPR) built tracks across Alberta and settlers began arriving to start new lives and to cultivate the land. At the time, no one appreciated the fact that the rain on the plains was cyclical. Indeed, drought came to the region again, limiting the expansion of agriculture from the mid 1880s to the mid 1890s.

Wheat fever struck Alberta in the late 1890s, driven by the end of a drought, railway expansion, and increased settlement. World War I also fueled demand for wheat, with prices reaching a record high of $2.31 a bushel in 1919.

The years between World Wars I and II were difficult for local farmers. Two cycles of depression and droughts brought widespread misery to rural Albertans, forcing some to abandon their land. After World War II, however, the economy stabilized and farmers once again found profit in the land. Crops diversified, thanks in part to an extensive irrigation system which had developed during the late-19th-to-mid-20th century. Irrigation allowed Alberta farmers to cultivate everything from oil seeds to small fruits.

This page: Bins store freshly harvested Alberta grain. Opposite page: A combine moves through a wheat field in Millet. Alberta farmers produced a record 8.5 million tonnes of wheat in 2005.

This page: The Knight Sugar Company factory in Raymond, pictured here in 1904, is credited with introducing the sugar beet industry to Alberta. Opposite page: Blooming canola creates a sea of gold on a Longview farm. In 2005, Alberta's canola production reached an all-time high, climbing to to 3.6 million tonnes, a 25 percent increase over the previous year.

Sugar beets and potatoes, in particular, flourished with the arrival of irrigation. Today the Taber region is home to a sugar beet processing plant owned by Montreal-based Rogers Sugar and to a potato processing plant operated by Lamb Weston, a division of ConAgra Foods in Nebraska. McCain Foods Limited, based in Florenceville, New Brunswick, operates a large potato processing plant near Coaldale.

While wheat has retained its dominant position in Alberta agriculture, other crops such as tame hay, barley, and canola are also grown in large quantities. In fact, the province led the country in barley and canola production in 2004.

A Taste of Alberta

For more than a century, Alberta's dairy and milling industries have added flavor to the local economy.

In the late 1800s, local farmers produced milk and butter for Albertans, but by the early 1900s, dairies and creameries had been established to cater to the growing demand for dairy products.

Private companies dominated Alberta's dairy industry until the early 1920s, when farmer cooperatives were created to collect, process, and market milk products. These

Photos by
A. Greene
Calgary

Churn-Room.

This page, left: Butter is churned at a Calgary creamery in 1914. This page, right: Stocked grocery shelves offer milk, one of Alberta's top dairy products. Opposite page: A wagon loaded with flour from an Edmonton miller heads to market in 1935.

cooperatives, which bought and consolidated many of Alberta's independent dairies and creameries, were a powerful force in the industry for nearly 70 years.

In the 1990s, multinational corporations replaced cooperatives as the central force in Alberta's dairy industry. Today Lucerne Foods, a subsidiary of Canada Safeway in Calgary; Italian dairy company Parmalat; and Saputo, of Montreal, are the three largest dairy firms operating in the province. Lucerne's two plants in Edmonton produce fluid milk and cultured products such as ice cream and yogurt, while Parmalat's Lethbridge plant manufactures yogurt, cottage cheese, and sour cream. Parmalat's Calgary plant processes fluid milk and ice cream as well. Saputo, which has operations in Calgary, Edmonton, Glenwood, Wetaskiwin, and Red Deer, produces everything from condensed milk and creamers to butter and cheese.

Some small companies have weathered changes in the industry, including Foothills Creamery in Calgary, which was founded in 1969 and manufactures cheese, butter, ice cream, and frozen yogurt.

Alberta's milling industry has also undergone significant changes since a grist mill was first established at St. Albert Mission in the 1860s. As demand for wheat skyrocketed

in the 1890s, more sophisticated mills were built in Calgary, South Edmonton, and Medicine Hat. Between the 1890s and 1920s, Canadian and American milling companies also built plants in these cities, and Calgary and Medicine Hat became Alberta's main centres for the industry.

The Depression had a long-lasting impact on Alberta's milling industry.

By the early 1950s, many of the smaller mills which had operated in the province closed down or were converted into cattle feed mills to serve the local area.

Today Alberta's wheat flour exports are valued at $7.6 million annually, and the province is home to 10 flour mills and 60 wholesale baking companies. Leading millers include Ellison Milling Company in Lethbridge and

Schroeder Milling in Camrose. Established in 1906 and owned by Parrish and Heimbecker of Winnipeg, Ellison Milling is the province's oldest surviving milling company. Schroeder Milling, founded in 1968, is best known for producing the Sunny Boy brand of cereal.

Timber Trade

Stretching along the eastern slopes of the Rocky Mountains and blanketing

the northern portion of the province, Alberta's forests cover close to 60 percent of its land. Since the late 1700s, when Alberta's trees provided timber for fur-trading outposts, forests have played an integral role in the province's development.

John Walter, a Scot from the Orkney Islands, was one of the first people to establish sawmilling operations in Alberta. In 1870, he came to Fort Edmonton to work as a boat builder for the Hudson's Bay Company. After fulfilling the terms of his employment contract in 1875, he moved to a farm across the North Saskatchewan River and immediately put his boat-building skills to use constructing scows and ferries. As Edmonton grew, Walter took the profits from his boat-building ventures and diversified into sawmills and timber cutting in 1894. He built a mill on the river flats at Edmonton and used the North Saskatchewan River to deliver logs from timber limits in the west.

Meanwhile, a consortium of Canadian and American interests was brought together in Calgary in the early 1880s to create the Eau Claire and Bow River Lumber Company. The company floated logs down the Bow River from timber limits west of Calgary.

Railway companies, coal miners, and settlers in Alberta had an insatiable

appetite for wood products during the late 1800s. Lumber was needed for railway tracks, trestles, and stations; for coal mine railway props and ties; and for homesteads.

Alberta's lumber production tripled in the 1930s, since winter logging income helped many farmers to survive. To ensure sawmill jobs stayed in the province, Alberta banned the export of raw logs during the Depression. The war years brought a huge increase in demand, and lumber

production in Alberta doubled between 1939 and 1945.

The federal government managed Alberta's forests between 1899 and 1930, during which time it created national parks along the eastern slopes of the Rockies. To control and report forest fires, the government built a system of trails, observation posts, and telephone lines in the 1920s.

The forest areas which were logged, on the other hand, had no

This page, right: In 1912, lumber is cut at a sawmill near the town of Legal. Opposite page: Lodgepole pines are transported for processing into lumber, plywood, and pulp.

program of reforestation, posing a threat to the forestry industry. To address the problem, in 1948 the Alberta government designated about 60 percent of the province as a green zone in which settlement was to be restricted. The following year, legislation was passed to create agreements with developers based on the sustained-yield principle. North Western Pulp and Power, headquartered in Hinton, signed the first Forest Management Agreement (FMA) with the Alberta government in 1951. By the late 1990s, 17 FMAs were in place for an area of about 20 million hectares.

Alberta's forestry companies today produce lumber, pulp, paper products, furniture, cabinets, and doors. Large businesses active in the province include Vancouver-based Canfor, which operates mills in Grande Prairie; Vancouver-based West Fraser Timber Company, which has 11 facilities in Alberta; and Kamloops-based Weyerhaeuser Canada, which has locations in five Alberta cities.

Alberta's land has been producing wealth since the first cow was sent to market, the first bushel of wheat was harvested, and the first tree was cut down for lumber. Despite the setbacks caused by the Depression, droughts, and the sudden closure of markets, the agriculture and food processing industries have emerged strong, with a greater diversity of products. Through replenishing forests, Alberta's forestry industry has shown a similar desire to renew itself and help grow the province's economic base.

Chapter Three

Powering the Economy

More than 300 million years ago, during the Devonian period, oil-bearing rock formed in what would later become Alberta. Subsequent periods of geological formation left the region with generous amounts of coal, natural gas, and oil sands. For more than a century, Albertans have found ways to tap into these energy sources and in doing so have transformed the provincial economy and its way of life. Alberta is now the world's third-largest natural gas producer and its ninth-largest oil producer. This powerful sector of the economy accounts for nearly 304,000 jobs, or about 18 percent of Alberta's total workforce.

King Coal

The first energy source for Alberta's homes, transportation system, and factories was coal. It was initially discovered in northern Alberta by explorer and mapmaker Peter Fidler in 1702, then in the Crowsnest Pass by both Father Jean de Smet in 1845 and by George Dawson, a geologist working for the Geological Survey of Canada, in 1878.

Large-scale coal mining began in Lethbridge in the mid 1880s, and by 1909 the city had become Alberta's largest centre for domestic coal production. From the 1880s to the 1910s, coal mines opened in Edmonton, Drumheller, and locations along the eastern slopes of the Rocky Mountains.

Alberta's largest coal field, discovered in the Crowsnest Pass by de Smet and Dawson, was yielding more than three million tons of coal annually by 1913. Most of this coal was sold to the Canadian Pacific Railway (CPR) to fuel locomotives. Coke ovens were erected at the turn of the century at Coleman, Lille, and at Leitch Collieries to supply smelters in the United States as well.

By the 1910s, Alberta's major coal fields had been established. The province became Canada's largest coal producer in 1918, when its 317 mines produced more than six million tons of coal. After 1918, however, coal production stabilized, and the industry

faced an uncertain future due to the rise of hydroelectricity and petroleum, high production costs, and to a market largely controlled by the railways. The CPR, which charged premium rates for carrying coal, insisted on low prices as a consumer, forcing coal companies to operate on a narrow profit margin.

World War II briefly rekindled the demand for coal as the pace of industry and commerce increased. Alberta coal production hit a peak in 1946, when a record nine million tons were produced by 200 mines.

The boom was short-lived. The coal industry experienced its most serious crisis in the 1950s when railways converted to diesel and natural gas use virtually eliminated the local coal market. In 1962, coal production had dropped to two million tons. Mines closed throughout the province and coal-based communities such as Nordegg became ghost towns.

In the 1960s and 1970s, new markets were found in Japan for metallurgical coal, and a domestic market

developed for thermal coal to drive power plants. The industry shifted to open-pit mining, which was highly mechanized and less labour-intensive. With the development of new markets and advanced mining methods, coal production soared. Today Alberta's nine mines produce close to 30 million tons of coal annually.

Luscar Ltd. and Fording, two companies which survived these periods of transition, dominate the Alberta coal industry today. Headquartered in Edmonton, Luscar traces its beginnings

to 1910 and is now Canada's largest producer of low-sulphur thermal coal. Calgary-based Fording, which was originally part of the CPR group of companies, formally came into existence in 1968. Today Fording holds a 60 percent interest in the world's second-largest exporter of metallurgical coal, Elk Valley Coal Partnership, of Calgary.

An Elusive Treasure

Canada's early dependence on oil from the United States and Venezuela made it critical to find oil within the country. In the 1870s, there were

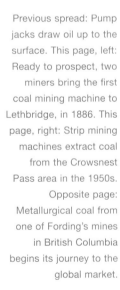

Previous spread: Pump jacks draw oil up to the surface. This page, left: Ready to prospect, two miners bring the first coal mining machine to Lethbridge, in 1886. This page, right: Strip mining machines extract coal from the Crowsnest Pass area in the 1950s. Opposite page: Metallurgical coal from one of Fording's mines in British Columbia begins its journey to the global market.

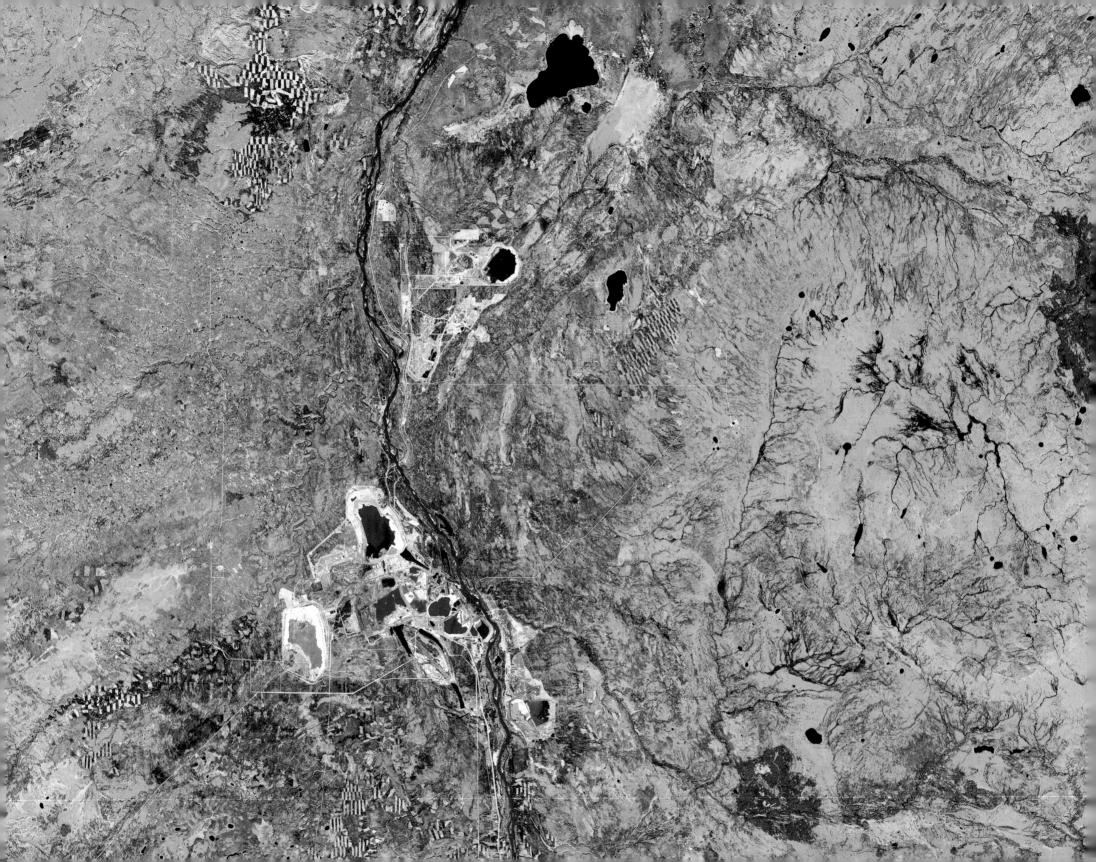

reports of oil seepages in what is now Waterton Lakes National Park, but it was not until 1902 that anyone attempted to extract it. That year, the Rocky Mountain Drilling Company drilled a well at Cameron Creek and struck oil. Initially, the well produced up to 350 barrels a day, and Alberta's first petroleum boomtown developed at the site. But neither this well nor seven others resulted in steady production, and the town was abandoned.

Following the initial discovery of oil in the south, exploration activity shifted north to Athabasca, where oil sands, noted by explorer Alexander MacKenzie in the late 1700s, held

MINING **OIL** FINANCE

Western Examiner

Vol. XXI No. 42   THE WESTERN EXAMINER, CALGARY, SATURDAY, FEB. 22, 1947   Price 10 Cents

At Birth of New Alberta Oil Field

IMPERIAL LEDUC No. 1 WELL—Discovery for a second major Alberta oil field, blowing out its huge billow of burning oil and heavy smoke when the well was completed as a big producer last week.

the promise of petroleum treasure. Attempts to extract the oil from these sands began in 1906, but prospectors' efforts were not fruitful.

The search for oil in Alberta during the interwar years had limited success—the most important find was natural gas and naphtha, a light oil condensate, in Turner Valley, in 1914. Another drilling boom was triggered, however, in 1936, when Turner Valley

Royalties' No. 1 well hit oil in Turner Valley. The Turner Valley oil field remained Canada's most important until 1947. Heavy oil was also discovered in Wainwright in 1925 and in Lloydminster in 1939. In the Fort McMurray area, prospectors focused on locating bitumen rather than oil pools.

Despite these modest discoveries, the Athabasca oil sands remained the best prospect for developing oil

in Alberta until 1947, when Imperial Oil, a company from Toronto, struck black gold at Leduc. On February 13th, Imperial Oil arranged to have the public watch the first oil coming out of one of its wells. What they witnessed that day was the birth of the oil age in Alberta.

Imperial Oil immediately drilled a second well close to the first to determine the extent of the field. This well

This page, left: The *Western Examiner* heralds Imperial Oil's landmark discovery at Leduc in 1947. This page, right: An Imperial Oil derrick at Cold Lake receives some maintenance. Opposite page: Fort McMurray's oil sands glow brilliant purple on a U.S. Geological Survey image.

went deeper and struck the even more productive Devonian reef formation. Imperial Oil was then joined by American and British oil companies in Alberta's great rush. These companies discovered oil at Redwater in 1948; Golden Spike in 1949; Fenn-Big Valley in 1950; Wizard Lake in 1951; Acheson, Bonnie Glen, and Westerose in 1952; Pembina in 1953; Swan Hills in 1959; and Rainbow Lake in 1965.

The conventional oil supplies found at Leduc eliminated any interest in recovering oil from Alberta's oil sands for the next 15 years. Then in 1962, the Alberta government regenerated interest in the oil sands when it initiated a policy to develop them. The following year, Sun Oil, now Suncor Energy in Calgary, invested nearly a quarter-billion dollars in the Great Canadian Oil Sands (GCOS) project at Fort McMurray. The facility, which was the world's first oil sands operation, came on stream in 1967. Around this time, a second consortium known as Syncrude initiated a research program to develop an oil extraction process for oil sands. In 1973, construction began on the Syncrude site near Fort McMurray, and the first barrel of oil was shipped five years later. Production steadily increased, with the billionth barrel sent down the pipeline in 1998. These ventures helped make Suncor and Syncrude two of Canada's largest energy companies.

Perseverance has made Alberta one of the world's largest oil producers, and more than half of Canada's conventional crude oil and all of its oil sands are produced in the province. About two-thirds of Alberta's oil is exported to the United States, representing a dramatic reversal of Canada's original dependence on American oil.

Several major oil companies are based in Alberta, including Petro-Canada and Shell Canada Limited. Established in 1975 and based in Calgary, Petro-Canada is engaged in oil sands and natural gas operations in Alberta as well as international oil and gas exploration. Shell Canada is also invested in Alberta's oil sands. The Calgary-based energy giant, incorporated in 1911, is a partner in the Athabasca Oil Sands Project. Imperial Oil, the company responsible for the discovery of oil at Leduc, also continues to operate in Alberta. In 2006, the Montreal-based company will move its corporate head office to Calgary.

A Natural Abundance

For many years the gas bubbling up along Sheep Creek near Turner Valley had attracted the attention of First Nations people and early ranchers. Legend has it that cowboys fried bacon and eggs over the gas seepages as they passed through the area on cattle drives. The first person to investigate the nature of this gas was rancher William Stewart Herron,

This page: Raw bitumen, a thick, black oil which is present in Alberta's oil sands, is poured at a Syncrude facility. Opposite page: Oil sands are processed at Syncrude's Fort McMurray operation, which has the capacity to produce 250,000 barrels a day.

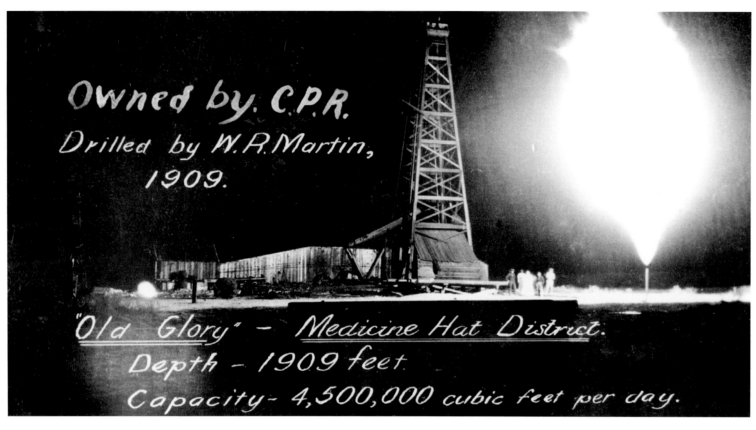

Owned by C.P.R.
Drilled by W.R. Martin, 1909.

"Old Glory" – Medicine Hat District.
Depth – 1909 feet.
Capacity – 4,500,000 cubic feet per day.

This page, left: Medicine Hat's "Old Glory" gas well spews a spectacular fireball into the sky in 1909. Opposite page: A plant near Millarville converts gas into a useable energy source.

who took the initiative to have it analyzed in the 1910s. The results prompted him to create Calgary Petroleum Products Company in partnership with Archibald Dingman, an experienced driller and promoter. The company began drilling in Turner Valley in 1913, and a year later, when one of its wells struck naphtha, speculation went wild.

Meanwhile, in the southeastern part of the province, a crew drilling for coal in Medicine Hat in 1891 found

out that the community was located on top of a gas field. Although no attempt was made to use the gas initially, it did have considerable amusement value—it became customary to entertain prominent visitors by "blowing off" a gas well, creating a deafening roar and a flame which leaped higher than the tallest building. Author Rudyard Kipling, who was one of the visitors treated to such a demonstration in 1907, later remarked that Medicine Hat "had all hell for a basement." By 1904, numerous reports of illness and

death caused by improper use of natural gas prompted the City of Medicine Hat to take over gas distribution.

In 1909, another major natural gas discovery took place nearby, when Eugene Coste struck gas near Bow Island. Coste's discovery led to the construction of a 270-kilometre pipeline to carry gas to Calgary via Lethbridge.

Further discoveries were made at Viking in 1914; Lloydminster on the Saskatchewan border in 1934; and

Jumping Pound, west of Calgary, in 1944. The discovery of oil at Leduc in 1947 also led to the establishment of gas wells. Explorations since 1947 have been aimed at mapping the extent of natural gas fields.

A number of energy companies have reaped the benefits of Alberta's generous natural gas resources. EnCana Corporation of Calgary, which got its start in the 1880s, is North America's leading natural gas producer. EnCana's natural gas fields

in southeast Alberta cover about 3.5 million net acres. Canadian Natural Resources Limited, headquartered in Calgary, has emerged as one of Canada's largest natural gas producers as well. Founded in 1989, the company has focused its natural gas and oil operations in western Canada, in the North Sea, and off the shore of West Africa. Calgary-based Husky Energy, established in 1938, is another major gas producer which has operations concentrated in western Canada. Shell Canada Limited, already a major oil sands producer, is also pursuing natural gas production; the company announced the discovery of a large natural gas field near Rocky Mountain House in 2004.

Electrifying Alberta

On a dark night in 1886, Peter Anthony Prince was walking along a Calgary sidewalk when he slipped and fell into the muddy street. At that moment, he decided that Calgary's streets needed to be lit by electric lights, and by 1889, the businessman had done exactly that. Five years later, the City of Calgary built its own electric light plant and established a municipal utility. In

1911, a group of businessmen in Montreal established Calgary Power Company Limited to provide power to Calgary, too. Between 1911 and 1954, Calgary Power built 11 water-driven electric generation plants on the Bow and Kananaskis rivers. In the 1920s, the company built transmission lines south to Magrath and Taber and north to Didsbury; by 1949, Calgary Power's system extended north to Westlock, south to the American border, east to Macklin, Saskatchewan, and west to Nordegg. The company was renamed TransAlta Utilities Corporation in 1981.

Electric light came to Edmonton for the first time in 1891. Electricity was provided by the Edmonton Electric Lighting and Power Company, which became Canada's first municipally owned electric light utility, in 1902. As demand for electricity increased, the city added generators and in 1931 operated the country's largest steam boiler.

International Utilities, headquartered in New York, was another early participant in the development of Alberta's electrical grid. In 1927, the firm created Mid-West Utilities Limited to operate small power plants in Vegreville, Lloydminster, Drumheller, Stettler, Hanna, and Grande Prairie.

Electricity came to Alberta's rural communities much later than to its

This page: Power lines transmit electricity in southern Alberta. Opposite page, left: A city-owned plant generates power for Edmonton in 1923.

Both pages: A safety
adviser checks tanks
storing chemicals
near Drumheller.

urban centres. In the late 1940s, rural electric cooperative associations, financed by farmers and low-interest government loans, slowly began supplying rural Albertans with electricity. The first such association formed in Blackfalds, in central Alberta, in 1947. By 1965, more than 260 rural electric cooperative associations had formed throughout the province. Many of these associations were sold to power utility companies in the 1970s and 1980s, but those which remained continue to play an important role in rural electrical distribution.

Following Alberta's deregulation of the electrical industry in the 1990s, Edmonton and Calgary's municipally owned utilities were reincarnated as private companies. In 1996, Edmonton Power was combined with other utility services to form EPCOR Utilities, and in 1998, the City of Calgary Electric System became ENMAX Corporation. TransAlta, headquartered in Calgary, continues to generate electricity, selling it to wholesale customers in North America and Australia. Alberta's utilities providers also include ATCO Electric in Edmonton, which serves customers in the northern and east-central part of the province.

Building on Hydrocarbons

For more than 50 years, Alberta's petrochemical industry has harnessed the raw elements of natural gas and oil to produce a wide range of products. The local petrochemical industry developed during World War II, when the Allied War Supplies Corporation built a plant in Calgary to synthesize ammonia from natural gas. The gas, taken from Turner Valley, was converted to make explosives. Following the discovery of oil at Leduc, Canadian Chemicals Company built a plant in Edmonton in 1953 to produce cellulose acetate for everything from yarn to fabrics. That same year, Canadian Industries completed a plant in Edmonton which utilized Alberta natural gas to produce polyethylene, used to make consumer goods such as packaging, pipes, and weather stripping.

Today NOVA Chemicals and Dow Chemical, both of which are headquartered in Calgary, are leaders in petrochemical manufacturing. A recently constructed ethylene cracker at Joffre, which is owned by both companies, is the largest single ethane-based cracker in the world. Dow Chemical's ethane-based cracker at Fort Saskatchewan is the second-largest in the world.

Alberta's diverse energy industry has gone through a fundamental change over the last century. Originally based on coal, the sector has expanded to encompass natural gas, oil, and petrochemical products. These bountiful energy sources have revolutionized life and commerce at home and abroad.

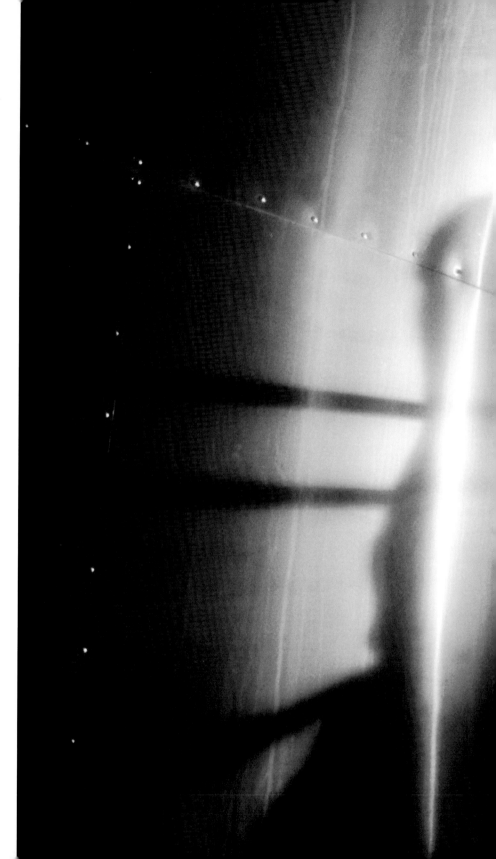

Chapter Four

The Knowledge Sector

Shortly after the province of Alberta was created, efforts were made to establish a superior postsecondary educational system. Plans began almost immediately to create the University of Alberta, and Dr. Henry Marshall Tory was recruited to be its first president, in 1908. Tory also played a major role in the founding of the Alberta Research Council in 1921, forging a vital link between education and research.

Nearly a century later, Tory's legacy of excellence is evident in Alberta's educational system and research community—the province boasts four universities, two technical institutes, 23 colleges, and some of the country's leading research centres. The synergy between research and education has also led to a burgeoning local biotechnology industry.

Expanding Minds

The first sitting of Alberta's Legislative Assembly in 1906 laid the foundation for the new province, including the creation of a first-class public university. Strathcona, which later became part of Edmonton, was selected as the site for the University of Alberta, and Dr. Tory, an esteemed educator, was hired as the university's first president. Classes began in 1908, with 45 students and five faculties; degrees were conferred on the first graduating class in 1912.

The school established a Faculty of Law in 1912 and faculties of Applied Science and Medicine in 1913. It also began offering noncredit educational services to people in all parts of Alberta through its Department of Extension. In 1933, the department established the Banff School of Fine Arts, which has since become the Banff Centre, a globally respected arts, cultural, and educational institution.

The U of A grew tremendously in the 1960s—enrollment more than doubled, and the physical size of the university more than tripled. The campus now encompasses 50 city blocks with more than 90 buildings and additional land off campus for research.

Today the university is one of Canada's top research institutions, with more than 400 research laboratories and several major agricultural

This page: Timothy Caulfield, research director of the University of Alberta's Health Law Institute, pauses from his work on health care legal issues. Opposite page, top: Students evaluate their classmates' work in a gallery at the Alberta College of Art and Design. Opposite page, bottom: A Northern Alberta Institute of Technology student demonstrates how to use a cutting torch.

research stations. In 2004, external research funding totaled more than $415 million. The school also leads the country in the number of 3M Teaching Fellowships, Canada's top award for undergraduate university teaching excellence.

Groundbreaking research, talented and esteemed faculty, and a breadth of educational programs have attracted students to the U of A. Alberta's first public university now has more than 35,500 students and offers more than 370 undergraduate and graduate programs.

Edmonton was selected in the early 1960s for another government-run postsecondary institution, the Northern Alberta Institute of Technology (NAIT). In 1962, NAIT enrolled its first class of 29 communication electrician apprentices. Four decades later, the institute offers about 250 programs to some 67,500 students. NAIT has also grown to eight campuses in Edmonton, Fairview, Grande Prairie, High Level, and Peace River.

The location chosen for the U of A was a great disappointment to the citizens of Calgary, who responded by creating Calgary College in 1910. The denial of degree-granting privileges to the college by the Alberta government in 1914, however, led to the college's demise in 1915. Fortunately, Calgary

received some solace when the government decided to create the Provincial Institute of Technology and Art there in 1916. For the first few years of its existence, the institute was predominantly used for the rehabilitation of returning war veterans, but following World War II—when the increased pace of industry created a demand for trained labour—the institute came into its own. Renamed the Southern Alberta Institute of Technology (SAIT Polytechnic) in 1960, the school now offers more than 2,300 courses ranging from petroleum engineering and geographic information systems to medical laboratory technology and respiratory therapy. More than 70,000 people attend SAIT each year.

The Alberta College of Art and Design (ACAD), originally part of

the Alberta Provincial Institute of Technology and Art, was founded in 1926. The Calgary college became a fully independent institution in 1985 and is now the largest art college in the North American Great Plains region. About 1,000 students attend ACAD, which offers undergraduate studies in painting, sculpture, visual communication design, jewellery, media arts, and more.

Just four years after ACAD was established, Mount Royal College in Calgary became a junior college affiliated with the U of A. Founded in 1910 as a primary and secondary school, Mount Royal grew quickly. World War II veterans enrolled in large numbers in the 1940s, and by the 1960s, the college had to relocate its campus to accommodate the

influx of new students. Today Mount Royal offers more than 60 programs to approximately 13,000 students studying everything from business and communications to science and the arts.

The U of A expanded into Calgary in 1960, and the campus officially became the University of Calgary in 1966. From an initial enrollment of 4,891 students, the U of C has increased to almost 28,000 full-time students and more than 60 faculties and departments. The university is also home to more than 30 research institutes and centres investigating a wide variety of topics such as the Arctic, energy, petroleum engineering, the humanities, software research and development, and transportation.

Postsecondary institutions were created outside Alberta's major metropolitan centres as early as 1907, when Canadian University College, a Seventh-day Adventist school, was established in Leduc. The college moved to Lacombe two years later and became a junior college in 1919. Today Canadian University College has 400 students and offers more than 20 undergraduate and certificate programs.

Augustana University College in Camrose opened as a Christian secondary school as well, in 1911. The liberal arts college began

offering university courses in 1959, when it became affiliated with the U of A, and it became Alberta's first private university in 1985. Augustana, which has about 1,000 students, was designated a faculty of the U of A in 2004.

Olds, Claresholm, and Vermilion were selected as sites for agricultural colleges in 1913 by the Alberta Department of Agriculture in an effort to promote knowledge of

sound farming methods. Though the Depression forced the closure of the school at Claresholm in 1932, both Olds College and the Vermilion School of Agriculture survived the difficult period. Alberta's largest agricultural school, Olds College graduates about one-quarter of English-speaking agricultural diploma recipients in Canada. It also offers courses in fashion, computerized office administration, and satellite technology. The Vermilion

School of Agriculture, which changed its name to Lakeland College in 1975, has approximately 1,300 students who study agricultural sciences, business administration, emergency services technology, and several other subjects.

The province's public university system expanded to Lethbridge in 1967, with the founding of the University of Lethbridge. More than 8,000 students today attend the

This page: Agribusiness majors at Olds College collaborate on a project. Opposite page, left: In 1927, Olds College students gather for their tractor class. Opposite page, right: Fountains greet visitors to the main administrative facility of Athabasca University.

university, which offers more than 150 programs through six faculties and schools.

Athabasca was chosen as the new location for Athabasca University (AU), Canada's leading distance-education university, in 1984. That year, AU moved its campus from Edmonton, where it was founded in 1970. The university offers bachelor's and master's degrees, plus university certificates.

In Service of the Community

Publicly funded colleges offering university transfer courses began with the establishment of Lethbridge Community College (LCC) in 1957, Canada's first such institution. In the first year of LCC's existence, approximately 36 students attended the college—now it serves more than 7,000 students each year who are trained in more than 50 programs.

Between 1964 and 1971, similar institutions were launched in Red Deer, Medicine Hat, Grande Prairie, and Edmonton. Red Deer College, the first of this group, opened its doors in 1964. Today more than 20,000 students attend the school. Medicine Hat College, founded in 1965, has grown to two campuses, in Medicine Hat and Brooks, and a student body of more than 14,000. Established in 1966, Grande Prairie Regional College caters to more than 10,000 students through 13 certificate and diploma programs and more than 20 degree route options. Grant MacEwan College, founded in Edmonton in 1971, is Alberta's largest college, with more than 40,000 students. MacEwan offers 74 programs of study.

Vocational education was also an important part of the educational agenda for the Alberta government in the 1960s. Between 1965 and 1970, a regional system of vocational colleges was created, primarily in northern Alberta. The institutions which have evolved from that system include NorQuest College in Edmonton, Bow Valley College in Calgary, Keyano College in Fort McMurray, Portage College in Bonnyville, and Northern Lakes College in Slave Lake.

NetMedia, which produces computer-
based training materials and operates
high-speed computer networks. ARC
now employs more than 500 scientists,
engineers, business managers, and support staff in five facilities in Edmonton,
Calgary, Vegreville, and Devon.

In the last 25 years, the Alberta
government has also established
organizations such as the Alberta
Heritage Foundation for Medical
Research and the Alberta Ingenuity
Fund to distribute money to Alberta
researchers. Since its inception
in 1980, the Alberta Heritage
Foundation has contributed more
than $780 million to biomedical
and health research, while the
Alberta Ingenuity Fund, created in
2000, has endowed a wide range of
scientific and engineering projects.

Exploring New Frontiers

In 1921, Canada's first provincial
research organization, the Alberta
Research Council (ARC), was created
by the Alberta government. Located
at the U of A, the ARC immediately
began working on documenting
the province's mineral and natural
resources. Five years later, the ARC
published the first geological map
of Alberta.

Finding a way to extract oil from
oil sands was another issue the ARC
tackled in its early years, and in 1929,
researcher Dr. Karl A. Clark patented
a hot-water process for separating oil
from the sands. This revolutionary
process laid the groundwork for con-
temporary oil sands extraction methods. In 1986, the organization moved
its headquarters from the university to
Edmonton Research Park, by which
time it was focused on bridging the
gap between fundamental research
and technology commercialization.
In 1993, the organization spun off
its first company, Calgary-based Axia

Centres of Excellence, which are partnerships between universities, the government, and industry, are joining Alberta's research community as well. In 1995, the Sustainable Forest Management Network was established at the U of A to raise awareness of scientific issues impacting Canada's forests. The centre informs policymakers and helps businesses revise or renew land management strategies. The Protein Engineering Network of Centres of Excellence (PENCE), also at the U of A, was created in 1990 to study protein engineering and proteomics, which is the identification of complete sets of protein and protein-protein interactions. The research being conducted by PENCE scientists may help in the treatment of everything from smallpox to cancer.

The U of A is also home to the National Institute for Nanotechnology (NINT), a $120 million institute focused on research at the nano, or molecular, level. Established in 2001, the institute employs researchers in physics, chemistry, biology, engineering, medicine, pharmacy, and informatics. NINT's research targets the integration of biological structures, such as proteins and lipids, with inorganic materials, such as metals and crystalline semiconductors.

The Next Level

Research has reached a new level of sophistication with the advent of biotechnology. Alberta's biotechnology industry has its roots in the early 1960s, when research programs were created at the U of A and the U of C. The first significant biotechnology company to be spun off from the U of A was Raylo Chemicals, in 1963. The Edmonton-based firm is now a division of German company Degussa Fine Chemicals and makes ingredients and intermediates for the pharmaceutical and biopharmaceutical industries.

Alberta's first human health drug companies developed in the 1970s

and 1980s. In 1977, Chembiomed was established in Edmonton to commercialize carbohydrate chemistry pioneered at the U of A. In 1991, Chembiomed's research programs were incorporated into the ARC, but their technology reappeared in 1994 when SYNSORB Biotech was created in Calgary. Today SYNSORB's products are focused on bacterial toxins in the gastrointestinal tract. Biomira, founded in 1985, was another of Alberta's first human health drug companies. Two decades after it was

founded, the Edmonton-based firm is a leader in immunotherapy and organic chemistry for the development of cancer therapeutics.

Alberta's biotechnology industry expanded rapidly in the 1990s. Public interest in biotechnology had increased, research at Alberta's universities had progressed, and a positive investment climate pervaded. During the 1990s, 27 new biotechnology companies were founded in the province, focusing on agricultural biotechnology, cancer therapeutics,

natural health products, and infectious diseases. Since 2000, 18 new biotechnology companies have been created in Alberta—nearly 20 percent of all active companies in the province. In 2005, Alberta was home to 61 biotechnology companies.

The history of education, research, and biotechnology in Alberta is bound together by people who had a vision of excellence. It is this comprehensive vision which has made the province a leader in education and science.

This page: A lab technician inoculates a petri dish with a bacterial culture. Opposite page: DNA is sequenced as part of the drug discovery process.

Building on the Frontier

Building the Alberta economy has long attracted professionals in the fields of engineering, architecture, and law. The skills of engineers have been applied to everything from Alberta's railway system in the 1880s to oil sands plants at the turn of the 21st century. Monuments to the talent of Alberta architects range from the ornate Alberta Legislature Building in Edmonton, completed in 1912, to the curvilinear St. Mary's Church in Red Deer, built in 1968. Over the years, lawyers have also helped shape the province's development.

Alberta's finance industry has its roots in the 1880s, when local banks offered credit to settlers who needed to buy land and machinery. Settlement also was the impetus for the development of the local real estate sector, which has experienced a series of boom cycles during the last 100 years.

Form and Function

One of the first professional groups to play a role in Alberta's development was land surveyors, who arrived following Canada's purchase of Rupert's Land from the Hudson's Bay Company in 1869. Their initial task was to lay out the grid which would divide the land into manageable blocks for use as farms or urban communities. While creating this grid, surveyors also determined the routes for Alberta's railway system, beginning with the Canadian Pacific Railway (CPR) in 1883, as well as rights-of-way for roads in the 1880s and Alberta's irrigation canals as early as 1893.

Many land surveyors were also trained as engineers and thus played a dual role in the construction of Alberta's railways, irrigation systems, and bridges. Some of the engineering projects these professionals worked on included the Bassano Dam, east of Calgary, built between 1910 and 1914; the aqueduct at Brooks, built between 1912 and 1914; the 1909 railway bridge across the Oldman River in Lethbridge; and the reinforced concrete bridge across the Bow River at Centre Street in Calgary, completed in 1916.

Peter Turner Bone was one of Alberta's first engineers. Born in Scotland, Bone moved to Alberta in 1883 to work as an engineer for the CPR. In 1892, he opened a private practice in Calgary and worked on a variety of projects, including the Calgary Irrigation Company system. In 1903, Bone embarked on the most important project of his career when he became assistant chief engineer for the CPR's irrigation project east of Calgary.

The separation between land surveying and engineering came in 1920 with the passage of the Engineering Profession Act, which led to the creation of the Association of Professional Engineers of Alberta. Only a member of this association could be designated as a "registered professional engineer." It has since become the Association of Professional Engineers, Geologists, and Geophysicists of Alberta.

There was little demand for engineers during the interwar period, though a few construction projects such as the Glenmore Dam in Calgary were completed. In the 1940s, however, engineers were needed to build war-related projects such as airports and the Alaska Highway. This increased demand

Previous spread: Coworkers chat on the way to the office in Calgary. This page, top: Peter Turner Bone, one of Alberta's first engineers, is pictured here in 1884. This page, bottom: A construction crew builds the Bassano Dam, circa 1910–1914. Opposite page: Water from the Bow River flows through the Bassano Dam.

was sustained by the postwar oil boom, which led to the construction of new roads, pipelines, refineries, and petrochemical plants.

The need for engineering services continues to remain high. Alberta's thriving engineering and geoscience sector now employs about 17,000 people in 5,000 firms. In fact, Alberta has the highest per capita ratio of engineers and geoscience professionals in Canada and one of the highest ratios in North America.

Today many Alberta engineering and geoscience firms are exporting services to other countries. Areas of specialization include the discovery and utilization of hydrocarbons, pipeline construction and operation, water resource management, thermal power generation and cogeneration, environmental engineering, public transportation infrastructure, and cold weather engineering. Companies involved in this kind of expertise include Stantec, which was founded in Edmonton in 1954 and now has more than 60 locations in North America and the Caribbean, and Focus Corporation in Edmonton, which opened in 1977 and today has more than a dozen offices in western Canada.

Designs for Living

Like engineers, architects have also had to ride the boom-and-bust nature of Alberta's economy. Architects first

This page, right: Blueprints for an office building are revised. Alberta has some 1,200 registered architects. Opposite page: Snow blankets the Alberta Legislature Building, which was completed in 1912.

set up practices in Alberta between the 1890s and 1910s, when they were in high demand to design residential, commercial, and institutional structures for the province's rapidly growing cities. One of the landmark buildings of this period was the Alberta Legislature Building. Designed by provincial architect Allan Merrick Jeffers and finished in 1912, the beaux arts–style building

incorporated granite from Vancouver Island, paskapoo sandstone from the Glenbow quarry near Calgary, and sandstone from Bedford, Indiana.

The minimal amount of construction between World Wars I and II made it difficult for Alberta architects to find work. One architect, however, left an indelible mark on the province during this time. Peter Rule, who

This page, left: Designed by the architecture firm of Rule Wynn and Rule, the Deer Lodge provides a cozy retreat for visitors to Lake Louise in 1963. Opposite page: The Edmonton Space Sciences Centre, created by Alberta architect Douglas J. Cardinal in 1984, hovers over the landscape like a space-ship about to take off.

worked as a building inspector for Alberta Government Telephones (AGT), designed the distinct clinker brick AGT offices in the 1920s which became a familiar sight in many small towns.

The pace of work picked up for Alberta architects in the 1950s, and the firm of Rule Wynn and Rule, in particular, played an important role in the development of modern architecture in Alberta over the next decade. In the 1960s, the Edmonton-based firm designed Elveden Centre in Calgary for the Irish brewing company Guinness. It was the first modern skyscraper to be built in Calgary.

One of Canada's most celebrated architects, Douglas J. Cardinal, began practicing in Edmonton in 1964. Just four years later, Cardinal earned acclaim for St. Mary's Church in Red Deer, whose unique design featured undulating shells. Though Cardinal eventually moved his office to Ottawa, he continued to design buildings in Alberta such as Grande Prairie Regional College in 1976, the Ponoka Government Services Centre in 1977, and the St. Albert Civic and Cultural Centre in 1983.

Today there are approximately 1,200 registered architects working in Alberta and more than 400 registered architecture firms. Two of the

largest are BCMP Architects in
Calgary, established in 1992, and
Cohos Evamy in Calgary and
Edmonton, founded in 1960.

Justice Served

In 1874, the North-West Mounted
Police was dispatched to southern
Alberta to establish law and order.
Led by James Macleod, the police
began the task of curtailing American
whiskey traders in the area. Macleod

then established a fort near the
Canadian Rockies bearing his name
in 1874 along with a fort in Calgary
in 1875. He was given judiciary
powers as the first of three stipendiary
magistrates of the North-West
Territories and was appointed to the
Supreme Court of the North-West
Territories in 1887.

Other pioneer lawyers in Alberta's
early days included Frederick Haultain,

James Lougheed, and Alexander
Cameron Rutherford. Haultain, who
came west from Ontario in 1884 to
practice law at Fort Macleod, served as
premier in the North-West Territories
Government and led the fight for
responsible government. Rutherford
established a practice in South
Edmonton in 1895 and became
Alberta's first premier in 1905.
Lougheed, who opened a law firm
after his arrival in Calgary in 1883,

was the Conservative leader in the
Senate from 1906 to 1921 and held
various positions in the federal cabinet
between 1911 and 1921. Lougheed's
grandson Peter, also a lawyer, was premier of Alberta from 1971 to 1985.

Lawyers continue to influence
Alberta's growth. With more than
7,400 lawyers in Alberta today, the
legal community is robust. One of
Alberta's most well-known firms is

Bennett Jones, established in Calgary in 1922. Now one of western Canada's largest law firms, Bennett Jones has additional offices in Edmonton and Toronto. Fraser Milner Casgrain, which traces its beginning to 1887, has offices in Calgary, Edmonton, Vancouver, Montreal, Ottawa, Toronto, and New York.

Financing Development

Alberta's first banks were private partnerships, one of the first of which was between Regina banker Fred G. Smith and Calgary doctor James Delamere Lafferty. Together, the two businessmen created Lafferty and Smith in Calgary in 1885. Around this time, chartered banks were being established in

Alberta as well. In 1886, Toronto-based Imperial Bank of Canada opened Alberta's first chartered bank branch in Calgary. By 1914, 16 Montreal- and Toronto-based banks had established branches in Alberta, virtually eliminating all of Alberta's private banks. The chartered banks were quickly joined by mortgage and loan companies, all of which provided short-term credit to settlers.

Alberta's network of financial institutions expanded through the early 1920s in response to the prosperity of the agriculture industry. The annual harvest was thus of great interest to bank managers, since its success would influence farmers' ability to pay their debts. A drought in

southern Alberta from 1918 to 1923 and a sudden decline in the price of wheat in 1920 created the first financial crisis. Companies in Alberta's financial sector were forced to declare bankruptcy and many bank offices closed. The cycle of drought and depression repeated itself in the 1930s, resulting in a second financial crisis.

In 1935, Albertans elected William Aberhart the leader of the Social Credit movement. Premier Aberhart devised a banking reform program which, though never successfully implemented, did leave a legacy in the form of Alberta Treasury Branches. Originally intended to administer Aberhart's program of Non-Negotiable Transfer Vouchers, the system evolved into a more traditional banking

institution, ATB Financial, in 1943. Today based in Edmonton, ATB has assets of $16 billion and is Alberta's largest financial institution. The bank serves more than 600,000 Albertans through 150 branches.

Canadian Western Bank, another top Alberta-based financial institution, opened its doors in 1988. Headquartered in Edmonton, it now has more than 30 branches in western Canada.

Chartered banks, which have been in Alberta since the 1880s, continue to be an important part of the financial sector. The Bank of Montreal, TD Bank, CIBC, Scotiabank, the Royal Bank of Canada, and the National Bank of Canada all have a major presence in Alberta.

Alberta's urban communities first appeared along its railways, with construction booming from the mid-1890s to the early 1910s. The pace of development led to rampant land speculation, which created extensive areas of subdivided—but undeveloped—land around virtually all of the province's urban communities.

The wealth to be made from land development at this time attracted entrepreneur Freddie Lowes, who came west to Calgary in 1899 as an employee of the Canada Life Assurance Company. In 1906, he went into business for himself and created western Canada's biggest real estate company. In 1912, Lowes undertook his most ambitious project when he spent $50,000 washing 100,000 cubic yards of earth from Calgary's Mission Hill into the Elbow River, making possible the luxury suburb of Roxborough.

Just a year later, however, Alberta's real estate market collapsed. Some revival in development occurred in the late 1920s but came to an end with the Depression in the 1930s. Fortunately, the post–World War II oil boom reinvigorated the real estate market as the demand for industrial sites, commercial space, and homes expanded. By the early 1980s, the downtown cores of Calgary and Edmonton had been rebuilt with modern skyscrapers.

In the 1980s, Edmonton's Triple Five Group set the standard for suburban shopping centre development when it began the first phase of the West Edmonton Mall in 1981. The mall has since expanded into the world's largest entertainment and shopping complex, with more than 800 stores, as well as amusement parks, aquariums, and more than 100 restaurants. In the 1990s, Triple Five developed the largest retail complex in the United States, the Mall of America in Bloomington, Minnesota.

Today Alberta is in another cycle of building construction, with nearly 150,000 people employed in the construction sector and 2,000 construction firms. Leading construction companies include PCL, which was established in Edmonton in 1906, and Loram International in Calgary, which has been in business since 1898.

The skills of surveyors, engineers, architects, lawyers, and real estate developers have had a lasting effect on Alberta's physical and social landscape. Local financial institutions have played an important role as well by providing much-needed capital for growth.

This page, left: An exact replica of Christopher Columbus's *Santa Maria* sails at one of West Edmonton Mall's water attractions. Opposite page: Edmonton's skyline reflects the city's tremendous growth since it was incorporated as a town in 1892.

Part Two

Partners in Progress

Profiles of Companies and Organizations

Alberta Cities

Profiles of Companies and Organizations

City of Medicine Hat

With 2,513 hours of sunshine a year, Canada's sunniest city also has the lowest municipal tax and utility rates in Alberta, a thriving economy, and a captivating culture tied to its plains heritage, making it a 'community of choice' for living, working, and playing.

Above left: The scenic South Saskatchewan River is the backdrop for Medicine Hat. Above right: Enclosed in glass to take advantage of sunny days (of which there are no shortage in Medicine Hat), city hall has a gorgeous, elaborate flower garden.

The sunniest city in Canada, Medicine Hat offers a quality of life that is hard to match. The number of residents now exceeds 56,000 people. The friendliness of its residents, its great outdoor leisure, and its thriving economy make Medicine Hat a great place to live, visit, and do business.

Founded in 1883, "the Hat" lies on the plains of southeast Alberta, less than 100 kilometres from Saskatchewan. The entrepreneurial spirit of Medicine Hat's forefathers drove its residents to invest in and develop gas and electrical utilities in the early 1900s. Careful stewardship of these resources and strategic business decisions have since provided a quality of life that is hard to match. Medicine Hat has the lowest combined municipal property taxes in Canada and the lowest utility rates in Alberta.

The scenic South Saskatchewan River valley is the backdrop for the city, which has more than 90 kilometres of hiking and biking trails and 250 hectares of parks. There are six first-class golf courses and many sport and leisure centres; in fact, Medicine Hat has more recreation centres per capita than most other Canadian cities.

Flourishing arts, culture, and music also enliven the city. In 2005, the Esplanade Arts and Heritage Centre opened. The Esplanade celebrates and showcases the spirit of Medicine Hat with its museums, archives, art gallery, two performing arts theatres, and discovery centre.

Medicine Hat is a major urban centre in southeast Alberta. Its diversified manufacturing sector produces industrial and consumer goods for domestic and export markets. The area's economic stability also hinges on its strong agriculture sector.

Medicine Hat takes great care to ensure that its schools deliver the best possible education for its young people. Medicine Hat College offers more than 40 full-time programs. Certificate and diploma programs include business, technology, early childhood development, travel and tourism, rehabilitation services, nursing, police and security, and visual communications. University transfer programs include education, engineering, science, and preprofessional programs.

With abundant sunshine, warmth, friendly people, and entrepreneurialism, Medicine Hat is a choice community brimming with opportunity.

Saamis teepee, Medicine Hat

The City of Edmonton

The northernmost major city on the continent, Edmonton, the 'Gateway to the North,' is where Alberta's fertile farmlands, vast natural resources, high technology, and flourishing culture intersect, making this capital city the gateway to Alberta's future prosperity as well.

The city of Edmonton is proud to be Alberta's capital, especially on its centennial anniversary.

This is an amazing and exciting time for Edmonton, with records being broken and benchmarks being set in construction, new jobs, business, research, education, art, and culture.

Over a million people live in Greater Edmonton—Canada's largest and most cosmopolitan northern city. And each person contributes to Edmonton's international reputation for excellence in sports, culture, health care, and higher education.

Edmonton's leadership in nanotechnology, medical research, and engineering —among many other fields—is literally changing the world.

Edmonton residents are active participants in professional and amateur sports and proud and successful hosts of countless international athletic events. The city is internationally known for its festivals, which are

celebrated almost year-round. From folk music concerts and independent film festivals to fringe theatre and jazz performances and more— Edmonton claims some of the most attended and successful international cultural events anywhere, in some of the world's premier performance and display venues.

Entering the new century, Edmonton will present itself to the world—as a tourist destination, a research and education centre, and a prime location for immigrants bringing their skills and talents to a new country. Edmonton will continue to be a key strategic partner in the phenomenal

growth and industrial exploration of Alberta's north. The world will know the city as a place to invest, a place to meet and share ideas, a place to innovate, a hub for arts and cultural expression. In this, the New West, the world will know a smart city, an active city, a green, growing, and vibrant city.

Edmonton looks forward to the next hundred years and to serving others with generosity and a willingness to help anyone in need, whether close to home, across Canada, or around the world.

Edmonton is truly a capital with great reverence for its past and an even greater vision for its future.

Above right: The striking Muttart Conservatory, through which downtown Edmonton appears, houses sundry flora in its four glass pyramids, symbols of the city's union of nature and modernity. Above far right: Edmonton's city hall glows as night falls.

Edmonton Economic Development Corp.

A booming city like Edmonton, with a metropolitan population in excess of one million, needs clear, actionable economic goals to stay on a growth trajectory; this economic development group defines those goals and charts the course to meet them through support for business and tourism.

Since its formation in 1993, Edmonton Economic Development Corp. (EEDC) has helped bring significant economic success to Greater Edmonton. It was created when four organizations—Edmonton Economic Development Authority, Edmonton Research Park Authority, Edmonton Convention and Tourism Authority, and Edmonton Convention Centre Authority joined forces to bring cohesiveness to the region's economic growth priorities. Its vision is to have a measurable impact on the quality, sustainability, and diversification of the region's long-term economic growth.

Edmonton Economic Development Corp. (EEDC) markets Greater Edmonton to the world. It is responsible for regional economic development, regional tourism marketing, and the management of the Shaw Conference Centre and the Edmonton Research Park.

EEDC is guided by a volunteer board of directors made up of 15 community business leaders. Together they have established the following economic growth goals for Greater Edmonton's future:
- Increase tourism, conventions, and visitations
- Maintain and strengthen the resource-based economy
- Support opportunities for value-added resource industries
- Support and encourage a knowledge-based economy
- Create tangible value for established businesses
- Encourage a positive regional business and investment environment

EEDC manages three divisions to accomplish these goals: Economic Development, Edmonton Tourism, and the Shaw Conference Centre.

The Economic Development division markets the region's competitive advantages to attract business; retains business by helping at-risk firms and removing growth barriers; develops and strengthens industry clusters; supports knowledge-based businesses; and develops and manages the Edmonton Research Park.

The Edmonton Capital Region Tourism Partnership Council sets the course for EEDC's Edmonton Tourism division, which markets Greater Edmonton as a preferred destination for leisure travel, business travel, and film production.

EEDC's third growth engine is its sound management and promotion of the 82,000-square-foot, glass-tiered Shaw Conference Centre. With its world-class chefs, award-winning architecture, and gorgeous view of the North Saskatchewan River valley, the centre is ideal for conferences and other events. The centre has column-free exhibit space, 23 multi-purpose meeting rooms, and on-site banquet facilities. The stunning Hall D expansion, which was opened in March 2006, boosts the annual economic impact of the Shaw Conference Centre to $43 million.

EEDC is an organization unique in Canada that has successfully united Greater Edmonton's many economic development initiatives, continues to champion the region's economic advantages, and serves the region's business community with innovative and results-oriented programs.

Below, far left: A Canadian economic leader, Greater Edmonton offers all the urban amenities expected of a thriving metropolis while maintaining an affordable, clean, safe, and family-oriented environment for work and play. Residents are especially proud of Edmonton's 7,400-hectare river valley park system, which is the longest urban park in North America —almost 22 times larger than New York City's 341-hectare Central Park. Below left: Allan Scott, president and CEO, is credited with transforming EEDC into a best-of-class organization.

Education

Profiles of Companies and Organizations

St. Mary's University College

At this modern liberal arts Catholic college, students learn how to make a life, not just a living, by immersing themselves in scholarship and service; each student graduates a cognizant citizen committed to learning for life and living for the common good.

Above left: Dr. Terrence J. Downey serves as president of St. Mary's University College. Above center: The Catholic tradition of academic freedom and social justice—informed by learning, civility, and hope—is the guiding "light" of this modern liberal arts college. Above right: As such, St. Mary's' professors guide, support, and encourage every student to develop academically, spiritually, and compassionately.

In 2004, St. Mary's University College in Calgary graduated its first baccalaureates. Currently, this esteemed institution of higher learning is the only Catholic liberal arts college in western Canada. As one of Canada's newest degree-granting schools, St. Mary's treasures learning, civility, and hope.

In the Catholic tradition of academic freedom and social justice, St. Mary's teaches students of all faiths integrity, confidence, wisdom, and passion for the common good. Synthesizing faith and reason, the college inspires students to search for meaning, purpose, and truth.

St. Mary's stresses individual attention. Small classes let students ask questions, explore subjects in depth, and truly understand what they study. St. Mary's

hires professors who have not only mastered what they teach, but teach masterfully well. Students trust the faculty to inspire and stimulate creativity, cultivate talents and abilities, and stoke interest in things new and challenging. Faculty honor this trust, supporting and encouraging each student.

St. Mary's grants a four-year bachelor's degree with a major in English, a three-year bachelor's degree with a concentration in English, and a three-year bachelor's degree with a concentration in general studies. Aspiring teachers or education administrators can enroll in two post-degree programs: the Graduate

Diploma in Religious Education (GDRE), a 30-credit program, or the Religious Education Administration (REAP) certificate program.

For students planning to transfer and earn their degrees elsewhere, St. Mary's is a great place to start, with plenty of rigourous first- and second-year courses redeemable for credit at other universities. Wherever they go, students from St. Mary's have the cerebral and spiritual mettle to thrive.

In addition to outstanding academics, St. Mary's offers diverse clubs, a campus ministry, sports, and recreational

programs for students to build community outside the classroom. Six sport teams won championship banners in the 2003–2004 season—the second season St. Mary's teams competed in Alberta college leagues. And the Campus Ministry lets students live their faith by working with the poor and applying their unique talents to solve social problems.

Each St. Mary's student has an e-mail account, computer access, and the use of a modern networked library. The campus also has a bookstore, a learning centre, and counselling and health programs. Staff help students apply for awards and financial aid.

St. Mary's educates the whole person: heart, mind, body, and spirit, molding citizens who will make the world better. Terrence J. Downey, Ph.D., St. Mary's president, says, "We will inspire students to undertake responsible intellectual inquiry and to accept the challenge of working for the creation of a socially just world based on sound moral principles."

St. Mary's University College

University of Lethbridge

In 1967 this university began a journey from a small corner on a college campus to a prominent coulee landmark on the west side of Lethbridge—and what began as a dream has grown into an important institution, rich in history and respected across the globe.

University of Lethbridge

FIAT LUX

Right: The University of Lethbridge's University Hall was built from 1969 to 1972. Far right: Following the University of Lethbridge's first convocation ceremony in 1968, more than 500 students, graduates, faculty members, and community residents rallied in a parade to support the university in its right to locate the campus on the west side of Lethbridge.

In 1966, a government announcement proclaimed Lethbridge as the site of Alberta's third university, and the final steps were taken to turn a dream into reality. The highly debated and much-anticipated University of Lethbridge was the culmination of five years of effort by local citizens.

On September 11, 1967, more than 650 students attended the first day of classes at the new University of Lethbridge (U of L). This new liberal arts university found its first home on the campus of Lethbridge Junior College, which is now Lethbridge Community College. That same year, members of the first

board of governors took office, and shortly afterward, Dr. W.A.S. "Sam" Smith was appointed as the U of L's first president.

Throughout the fall of 1967 and the spring of 1968, university officials, Lethbridge citizens, and Alberta

government representatives continued the debate over a permanent site for the U of L. On May 18, 1968, following the university's first convocation ceremony, held at Southminster United Church, more than 500 students, faculty, and community members staged a protest march in support of autonomy for the U of L in the decision to locate the campus on the west side of Lethbridge. After a lengthy and often emotional debate, on May 31, 1968, a decision was made to relocate the campus from its original site to a new west side location.

By fall 1969, the U of L was ready to break new ground. On September 5, at a ceremony on the west bank of the Oldman River, Premier Harry Strom

turned the sod for the new campus. This would be the first of many sod-turning ceremonies over the coming decades as the U of L continued to expand and evolve.

After three years of construction, University Hall, uniquely designed by noted architect Arthur C. Erickson, took shape on the west side campus. The nine-level facility provides space for classrooms, laboratories, offices, student services, and resident housing. The new U of L campus was officially opened at a three-day event in September 1972.

Since those early days in the history of the U of L, enrolment has increased from 650 to more than 8,000 students. The university campus, along with west Lethbridge, has seen significant development. The university has grown to six faculties and schools of study; created additional campuses in Calgary and Edmonton; expanded its programming to offer graduate degrees in selected disciplines and professional programs; and has maintained its focus on student services, the liberal arts, and undergraduate education.

Although the U of L has grown considerably, its hallmark small class size has remained—ensuring that a U of L education is a personal experience for the student. (The average size of a U of L lecture in the 2004-2005 academic year was approximately 33 students.) Students at the U of L have the opportunity to study with world-renowned professors who hold distinguished records in their fields of research, and they can enhance their education through research and work experiences.

Throughout its history, the U of L has celebrated many achievements and received many accolades. Information about the U of L is provided by the university on its Web site (www.uleth.ca). Today, the U of L is one of Canada's leading primarily undergraduate universities and is internationally recognized for its commitment to students, inspired teaching, research excellence, and world-class technology.

"Since our founding, the University of Lethbridge has been guided by a singular vision—to build the most vital and engaging learning environment in Canada," says U of L president and vice-chancellor Dr. William H. "Bill" Cade. "Our success is a reflection of the many individuals who have played a role in our development. Nearly four decades of faculty, boards of governors, and senate members, administrators, employees, and more than 20,000 graduates have contributed to the emergence of this university as a world-class institution."

Above left: University of Lethbridge alumnus Marc Slingerland (at left) is shown with Dr. Marc Roussel, one of three professors in chemistry and biochemistry with whom Slingerland completed co-operative work terms. Slingerland was named 2003 Co-op Student of the Year by the Canadian Association for Co-Operative Education. Above right: The university's present-day campus was opened in 1972, showcasing University Hall, designed by Arthur C. Erickson to follow the natural landscape.

Lethbridge Community College

As Alberta celebrates its 100th birthday, this community college, a landmark in Canadian higher education, will celebrate its own 50th birthday in 2007, and it reflects with pride on having taught and trained thousands of people who have enriched the province and the country.

Above left: This bird's-eye view of Lethbridge Community College (LCC) shows its sprawling, scenic campus: modern buildings embellished with greenery, ample parking, and a gorgeous hill-country setting. Above right: For 7,000 students, the entrance to LCC is also the entrance to higher education and careers.

Lethbridge Community College (LCC)—Canada's first publicly funded community college— started out as Lethbridge Junior College in 1957 with 36 students. Since that bright beginning, it has matured into a prominent teaching and research institution in southern Alberta. Each year, more than 7,000 learners achieve academic and personal success at LCC.

Those first 36 students took university transfer or technical training courses under a handful of instructors. Today, more than 1,100 employees enable LCC to offer some 50 certificate, diploma, postdiploma, applied degree, and apprenticeship programs. The college's programs attract both local students and learners from other provinces and countries. Three of its most prominent offerings are criminal justice, environmental science, and nursing.

LCC has grown from a one-building campus of fewer than 10,000 square metres to one of almost 90,000-square-metres, encompassing 11 training and instructional buildings and 27 residence halls. The college's state-of-the-art Instructional Building, completed in 2002, is a showpiece designed to accommodate new ways of learning for students, individually and in groups.

The renowned Aquaculture Centre of Excellence at LCC, built in 1997, meets the growing need for applied research and trained scientists in western Canadian aquaculture and agriculture. (Southern Alberta is Canada's largest agricultural irrigation base.) The only education and applied research centre of its kind in Canada, it contains offices, laboratories, aquaculture space, greenhouses, and quarantine modules. LCC leases lab space to academic and private researchers as well.

Employers regularly seek out LCC graduates for their aptitude in fields that keep Alberta and Canada at the forefront of technology.

LCC students carry the spirit of Alberta with them wherever they go and embody its regard for education.

Deeply rooted in southern Alberta soil, Lethbridge Community College plays a vital role in the region, enriching the lives of thousands in its 50 years.

Concordia University College of Alberta

Established in 1921, Concordia University College of Alberta—which offers undergraduate and graduate degree programs—educates the mind and nurtures the spirit of its students.

Founded in 1921 in Alberta's capital city of Edmonton and operated by the Lutheran Church Canada, Concordia University College of Alberta emphasizes academic excellence taught in a caring environment. Concordia offers a wide range of undergraduate degrees in the arts and sciences, education, environmental health, management, and information systems security.

Concordia's first master's program, Master of Information Systems Security Management, is one of the first of its kind in Canada and opens new career paths to graduates of the program.

One of Concordia's greatest strengths is its size. With an enrollment of 1,900 in 2005–2006, Concordia offers its students the benefit of getting to know each other and their professors in a more personal and supportive learning environment. Dedicated faculty are committed to providing their students with an excellent education as they work together for the advancement of scholarship and research.

Concordia's new Hole Academic Centre, due to be opened in 2007, will encompass 56,000 square feet on four levels and will be the largest building on campus. All classrooms will be "smart" classrooms with state-of-the-art technology and room for program expansion. Dr. Richard W. Kraemer, President, says, "The building will provide enough space to serve our growing student body for many years to come."

The Hole Academic Centre is named in recognition of the outstanding generosity of Harry and Muriel Hole and their commitment to supporting Concordia's academic excellence and values.

In a recent survey of 15,000 postsecondary graduates from Alberta universities, private university colleges, and technical institutes, an astounding 99 percent of graduates expressed satisfaction with their overall Concordia education. They responded positively about the quality of the teaching, their educational experience, and the programs. The survey also revealed that 95 percent of graduates said they would recommend Concordia University College of Alberta to others.

Concordia's mission is to offer a quality education in a Christian context, and it serves people of all backgrounds. The university's nurturing atmosphere reflects Concordia's commitment to practicing the values of the Christian faith.

Dr. Judith Meier, Professor Emerita, History, describes Concordia this way: "What I love most about Concordia is that it has never become an institution. It is a 'people place,' a community where people are involved in one of the most exciting of human activities: learning."

Above left and center: Concordia University College of Alberta is one of Canada's largest accredited, Christian-based, degree-granting institutions. Above right: An architect's rendering shows the front entrance of Concordia's new Hole Academic Centre, which will be occupied in 2007.

Southern Alberta Institute of Technology (SAIT Polytechnic)

Providing relevant, hands-on applied learning designed to help students build careers, this established, globally recognized technical institute offers certificate, diploma, and applied degree programs in a wide range of fields and industries.

Above: The Southern Alberta Institute of Technology (SAIT Polytechnic) serves more than 70,000 registrants annually. Its main campus (shown here) is located in northwest Calgary, Alberta.

In 1916 Canada's first public technical school opened the doors of its temporary quarters in a former police and fire station adjacent to the Colonel James Walker School in southeast Calgary, Alberta. Named the Provincial Institute of Technology and Art, the technical school was established to provide training for returning World War I veterans. The institute offered classes in its makeshift facilities until 1922, when it was moved to its present location in northwest Calgary. Here, a three-storey red brick and sandstone building designed in the collegiate Gothic style was opened and became the Provincial Institute of Technology and Art's new home. It was shared by Calgary Normal School for the training of teachers. The building also housed the University of Alberta as an extension campus where university courses were offered to Calgarians, an arrangement that continued until 1960, when the University of Alberta in Calgary (now the University of Calgary) was established on its present campus. The institute's building, now known as Heritage Hall, was fully restored in 2001 and commands one of Calgary's best views of the Canadian Rocky Mountains and the city's downtown area on the banks of the Bow River.

From 1940 to 1946, during World War II, the institute's campus was taken over by the Royal Canadian Air Force and served as the No. 2 Wireless Training School of the Commonwealth Air Training Plan; during these years, the institute's classes were offered under the bleachers of the Calgary Stampede grandstand. When the institute returned to its wartime-transformed campus, it witnessed tremendous growth as demand for technicians and technologists soared in the ensuing years, and in 1948 apprenticeship training was begun.

In 1960 the institute was renamed the Southern Alberta Institute of Technology and became known as SAIT Polytechnic. In the years since the institute was established, SAIT Polytechnic's programs have grown to include courses leading to certificates, diplomas, and applied degrees, and apprenticeship training has expanded into dozens of disciplines. The institute

provides relevant, skill-oriented education in business, communications, construction, energy, engineering technologies, health, hospitality, manufacturing, tourism, and transportation. Each year, career training and skills upgrading are provided to more than 70,000 registrants.

SAIT Polytechnic's expertise in training students has experienced increased demand—by regional corporations for employee training, by First Nations for career development, and by global corporations internationally. SAIT Polytechnic serves more than 150 corporate clients,

including the top 10 Alberta energy exploration and production companies, and has created more than 350 custom-designed training packages, reaching all industry sectors.

International training is a growing area for this institution. Major successes of recent years include SAIT Polytechnic being selected as one of only three ExxonMobil training centres in the world, delivering energy-sector training to more than 35,000 Kazakhstan citizens since 1997. SAIT Polytechnic is currently providing training and education in 19 countries worldwide.

SAIT Polytechnic established a second campus in 1982 in Maryland Heights in northeast Calgary, and in 2004 it established its third Calgary campus with the opening of the Art Smith Aero Centre for Training and Technology, strategically located at Calgary International Airport. The centre is one of the premier aviation training facilities in Canada, featuring many specialized laboratories, an array of airplanes and helicopters, and a hangar large enough to accommodate the institute's Boeing 737-200, which is used for students' hands-on technical and aircraft-maintenance training.

SAIT Polytechnic programs are well respected among business leaders because the programs are designed with employers in mind. More than 1,000 business professionals, participating in 65 program advisory committees, provide advice and guidance to the institution. In addition, the SAIT Polytechnic board of governors hosts three Chairman's Circle meetings every year, at which more than 70 business and community leaders provide the institution with insights from their

respective fields on economic, technological, and societal trends, towards developing future SAIT Polytechnic programming.

Its comprehensive advisory system explains why SAIT Polytechnic enjoys one of Canada's best records of graduate employment—averaging 97 percent from 2001 to 2005. Additionally, this impressive record reflects the institute's numerous partnerships with leading national and international companies. The partnerships also have led to the establishment of 11 Centres of Technology Development on the institute's main campus, many of them unique in Canada. These specialized facilities are designed to ensure that SAIT Polytechnic graduates have the advanced skills that will enable them to realize their career ambitions and at the same time contribute toward the highly skilled workforce required by the economy.

At SAIT Polytechnic, students do not just learn about things—they learn how to do things.

Above: On the institute's main campus is Heritage Hall, a SAIT Polytechnic landmark. The institute also has a campus in Maryland Heights, in northeast Calgary, and a third campus—the Art Smith Aero Centre for Training and Technology—located at Calgary International Airport.

The Northern Alberta Institute of Technology

A cornerstone of the Alberta economy, The Northern Alberta Institute of Technology offers a variety of full-time and apprenticeship programs, part-time continuing education courses, and international education and business development—providing training that is innovative, relevant, and flexible.

Above left: On The Northern Alberta Institute of Technology (NAIT) main campus is the NAIT HP Centre for Information and Communications Technology, one of the world's most technologically advanced educational facilities. This leading-edge learning environment also gives businesses access to applied research and videoconferencing facilities. Above right: NAIT's first priority is the success of its students. Year after year, nine out of 10 NAIT students are employed within months of graduating.

The Northern Alberta Institute of Technology (NAIT) is a leader in technical training and applied education designed to meet the demands of Alberta's industries. Founded in 1962, the institute is a cornerstone of Alberta's economy and one of the largest postsecondary schools in the province. NAIT serves approximately 67,500 customers annually from eight campus locations: four in the Edmonton capital region and four in the thriving Peace River country, at Peace River, Grande Prairie, Fairview, and High Level, Alberta.

NAIT students can earn certificates, diplomas, and applied degrees in some 250 programs focused on the career fields of information technology; business; health sciences; hospitality; building sciences; resources and environmental management; and electrical, mechanical, and manufacturing technologies. In addition, NAIT is Canada's leader in apprenticeship training, providing technical skills to more than half of all the apprentices in Alberta and 17 percent nationwide.

NAIT graduates—more than 4,000 each year—help supply the skilled workforce required to support today's global, knowledge-based economy.

Providing Training Anywhere, Anytime

NAIT expertise goes well beyond its campus classrooms into offices, shops, and plants across the country and around the world. Proactive business and industry leaders look to NAIT to design, develop, and deliver training that is custom-tailored for their unique requirements. With close to four decades of experience in providing international education, NAIT has provided training in nearly 50 countries around the world.

Committed to Alberta's Bright Future

NAIT's vision, to be an outstanding technical institute committed to student success in a global economy, guides the institute in ambitious goals for the future. The long-term strategy includes a $500 million plan for campus expansion and human capital development to meet the needs of business, industry, students, and the economy.

As part of this strategy, plans are under way to expand facilities and programs to accommodate the training of 160,000 skilled workers—from accountants, welders, and ironworkers to magnetic resonance imaging (MRI) technologists —between 2010 and 2020. Such expansion will boost NAIT's training capacity by 35 percent in a number of disciplines and go a long way toward addressing Alberta's tremendous demand for a skilled workforce.

In addition, working with high schools and immigration authorities, NAIT is developing creative educational delivery methods and encouraging more young people to consider trades and technology careers.

All of these steps are designed to contribute to meeting the demand for a highly trained and productive workforce—the workforce that will help Alberta continue to shine in the years ahead.

Keyano College

What began in 1965 as a vocational centre to train workers for the oil sands industry has grown into Keyano College: a high quality, multipurpose educational facility offering a diverse range of exciting programs and services.

Keyano College is a first-rate post-secondary institution serving over 3,500 credit and 10,000 noncredit students each year. Employing a total of 122 faculty members and 181 administration and support staff, the college offers academic, trades, and workforce development programs.

Committed to providing excellent education, training, and services that will prepare students for the challenges of work and enhance personal growth, Keyano has highly qualified instructors and small class sizes ensuring students receive the personal attention they deserve. A strong athletics program, an impressive array of scholarships, and a variety of student housing options are just a few of the exemplary student services available.

Academically Keyano provides quality educational and training opportunities through three program divisions: Academic and Career Programs, Trades and Heavy Industrial Training, and Community and Upgrading Education. Keyano provides a diverse program

offering, ranging from Mine Operations to Nursing, Drama to University Studies, and Musical Instrument Repair to Environmental Technology.

Keyano's programs are provided through three campuses, four learning centres, and a community service centre. The main Clearwater campus, located in downtown Fort McMurray, is home to Keyano Theatre, Norm Weiss Arts Centre, and Keyano College Library, making the campus a cultural hub in Fort McMurray. To the south, in Fort McMurray's MacKenzie Industrial Park, is the Suncor Energy Industrial Campus, which is home to Keyano's Heavy Industrial programs and some trades; over 200 kilometres north lies the Fort Chipewyan Campus; and the Human and Community Services Centre is located in Edmonton.

But the growth does not stop there. In 2005, Keyano's Board of Governors

approved a Campus Development Master Plan that will serve as a blueprint for the growth and expansion of Keyano College during the next 25-year period, which will coincide with the investment and population increase expected in northeastern Alberta. By 2010, Fort McMurray's population is expected to climb to more than 100,000 residents.

The plan includes the construction of the Syncrude Sport and Wellness Centre as well as the expansion of the Trades and Technologies programs. Keyano will also be looking at expanding its certificate and diploma programs.

As Fort McMurray's population skyrockets, Keyano continues to grow and expand to help students meet the challenges of the future, while continuing to improve the quality of life in the Wood Buffalo region.

Above left: Keyano College offers Academic and Career, Trades and Heavy Industrial, and Community and Academic Upgrading programs in a highly diverse range. One example is its Musical Instrument Repair program, which is the only one of its kind in Canada. Above right: The Syncrude Technology Centre provides state-of-the-art classrooms, laboratories, and study space.

Energy
Profiles of Companies and Organizations

Prudential Steel

Superior manufacturing technology and unsurpassed service make Prudential Steel a leading North American steel pipe and tube producer and an essential participant in Alberta and Western Canada's energy services sector.

For more than 40 years, Prudential Steel has delivered oil country tubular goods (OCTG) and line pipe to energy companies as well as industrial pipe and tubing to builders and fabricators. Weathering the ups and downs of the famously erratic energy market, Prudential has produced and shipped more than two million tonnes of pipe and tubing in the last decade. Most of it is used in Alberta, the nation's energy center.

Oil and gas companies use Prudential's energy products OCTG (casing and tubing) in the wells they drill, and line pipe to transport oil and gas from well heads to refineries. The nearly 25,000 wells drilled in Western Canada in 2005 required more than one and a half million tonnes of energy products, and Prudential supplied a significant portion of that volume.

Steel arrives at the mill wound in coils up to 72 inches wide and weighing up to 32 tonnes. The mill's machinery uncoils the steel roll and cuts it into a number of strips that will be used to make various diameters of pipe. The strips are pulled through a series of forming rolls that gradually shape it into a tube. Continuous high-frequency induction welding using electrical energy fuses the edges of the steel to form a tube. The tube is then sized and cut to length, and a series of rigorous in-line quality assurance tests are conducted on each piece of tube.

Prudential, like few other companies in the world, can manufacture hydrogen-induced crack (HIC)–resistant pipes for sour gas (hydrogen sulfide) transmission.

Prudential believes strongly that each piece of pipe and tubing it makes is crucial to its customers' success. When customers require those products, they must have products they can trust at a fair price, from a supplier they can rely on—everything that Prudential delivers. Prudential builds quality into its products at each stage of the manufacturing process, starting with the best steel, using the latest technology, utilizing rigorous procedures, and employing a well-trained and experienced workforce to ensure unsurpassed quality in every product sold.

Prudential has established a culture of high quality and manufacturing excellence with its "Partners in Quality" programme. This programme continues the tradition established by Prudential's founders in 1966, when they constructed the first pipe mill to supply energy companies. Today, Prudential's 500-plus employees at the Calgary mill carefully monitor and control quality to make each piece of pipe and tubing worthy of the Prudential logo.

Above: Prudential Steel was established in 1966. In this historic photo (from left) are some of the original team members: Jim Wiles, sales and marketing; Norm French and Glen Peckham, management; unknown; Frank Finn, sales; and unknown. Right: Final visual inspection of finished OCTG tubing is performed. Every piece of pipe and tubing undergoes rigorous testing and inspection to meet Prudential's quality standards.

Manufacturing Milestones

Overall, Prudential fills orders by maintaining adequate inventories of finished goods and by scheduling its manufacturing to meet customer forecasts. The company listens to customers and responds to their needs—for example, Prudential has budgeted $4.3 million to increase OCTG threading capacity by 50 percent in 2006 to meet the growing drilling demand in Western Canada.

From the president's office to the shop floor, Prudential succeeds in delivering quality products and exceptional customer satisfaction. By valuing its employees, by developing strong relationships with its customers, and by recognizing its critical role in the energy services sector, Prudential Steel has established an excellent reputation as a leading North American steel pipe and tube company.

- 1966: Prudential Steel is conceived to supply line pipe to the growing energy industry in Alberta. Work begins on Mill #1 in Calgary. In 1967, its first year of operation, 22,000 tonnes are produced.
- 1975: Mill #2 in Calgary opens, raising capacity to 153,000 tonnes. Prudential starts making oil country tubular goods (OCTG).
- 1991: Prudential installs a central tool adjustment system, the first in North America, improving quality and selection.
- 1992: Prudential attains ISO (international) and CSA (Canadian) registration, the first mill of its kind to do so.
- 1994: Prudential begins a third mill; capacity increases to 240,000 tonnes per year.
- 1997: The new U.S. subsidiary, Prudential Steel Inc., plans a factory and distribution center in Longview, Washington, with capacity to make up to 100,000 tonnes of pipe per year.
- 1999: Mill #4, at Longview, starts making line pipe and OCTG under license of the American Petroleum Institute (API). Prudential approves a $7 million steel coil slitting centre at this mill.
- 2000: Prudential merges with Maverick Tube Corporation to create one of North America's largest manufacturers and suppliers of energy tubular products. Prudential plans construction of a new premium pipe threading line in Calgary.
- 2004: The original 1966 mill, Mill #1, is refurbished and modernized, increasing overall capacity in Calgary to 450,000 tonnes.
- 2005: Prudential introduces PS100-grade casing as a cost-effective alternative to alloy casing products, a first in the energy pipe business.
- 2006: Prudential approves the installation of a new threading line to meet Western Canada's growing energy sector demand. Threading capacity will be increased by 50 percent.

Far left: Prudential Steel manufactures a great variety of high quality pipe and tubing products for the energy services sector. Top left: Pipe is stenciled with information which provides full traceability for each piece of pipe and tubing produced. Top right: This leading company employs well-trained, experienced workers. Here, Ron Dulmadge, superintendent metallurgical testing laboratory, tests samples of steel used in manufacturing Prudential's high quality products.

BG Group plc

This rapidly growing company has operations on five continents and expertise across the gas chain, with the vision to be the leading natural gas company in the global energy market, operating responsibly and delivering outstanding value to its shareholders.

BG Group has a long history in the discovery, extraction, transmission, distribution, and supply of natural gas to consumers worldwide. Headquartered in the United Kingdom, the company has operations in over 20 countries, located in five global regions—North America and the Caribbean; South America; Europe and Central Asia; the Mediterranean basin and Africa; and Asia Pacific.

In 1997, after a demerger, British Gas plc was renamed BG plc, and a financial restructuring in 1999 created the new parent company, BG Group. BG Group has a reputation for engineering and technical excellence, combined with the commercial skills needed to supply the growing demand for natural gas in markets worldwide.

BG Group has expertise in all aspects of natural gas and operates in four business segments. Its exploration and production business is central to its activities. Liquefied natural gas (LNG), transmission and distribution, and power generation form the company's

downstream activities and enable delivery of natural gas to the consumer. In 2005, BG Group had revenues and other operating income of GBP 5.7 billion.

BG Canada is part of BG Group's North America and Caribbean region. The region includes Canada, the United States, and Trinidad and Tobago. BG Group is the leading importer of LNG to the United States, with an approximately 37 percent share of the market. BG Group has been operating in Trinidad and Tobago since 1989 and continues to reinforce its position as a major natural gas player in the country. Additionally, BG Group is a partner in the Atlantic LNG Company of Trinidad and Tobago, which operates one of the largest liquefaction plants in the world.

The strategy for success at BG Group, as an integrated natural gas company, is to deliver sustainable growth to shareholders through an approach that capitalizes on its skills and experience. BG Group combines a deep understanding of gas markets with

strong industry skills in finding and commercializing gas and in project delivery. This enables it to access competitively priced resources and bring them to market quickly and cost effectively and to create value across the gas chain. Additional information is provided by BG Group on its Web site (www.bg-group.com).

Corporate responsibility at BG Group encompasses the highest standards of business conduct, world-class treatment of employees and contractors, good relations with communities, and

exemplary performance in sustaining the environment.

The benefits of natural gas are valued around the world. Natural gas is competitively priced, can be found in abundance in a wide variety of geographic areas, and is the cleanest of the fossil fuels and the least harmful to the environment. BG Group's position as an industry leader and a responsible corporate citizen gives the company a wealth of opportunities for continued growth as natural gas increasingly becomes a fossil fuel of choice worldwide.

BG Group plc connects competitively priced natural gas supplies to high-value markets worldwide. Above left: BG Group is a partner in and the operator of the Armada platform, which produces gas in the United Kingdom (UK) central North Sea. BG Group has one of the most significant exploration and production businesses offshore the UK. Above right: The natural gas liquefaction plant at Idku, Egypt, is operated by Egyptian Operating Company for Natural Gas Liquefaction Projects S.A.E., a company in which BG Group holds a 35.5 percent interest.

BG Canada Exploration and Production Inc.

This company is in the business of oil and gas exploration and production in Canada, with a strategy based on developing its existing assets located in Alberta and British Columbia, expanding into new areas, and continually striving to operate safely and responsibly in all its activities.

BG Canada Exploration and Production Inc. is part of BG Group plc, a global natural gas business. BG Canada's business is the exploration, development, and marketing of natural gas and oil. BG Canada started operating in Canada in 2004 when BG Group acquired El Paso Oil and Gas Canada Inc. BG Canada's assets at the end of 2005 covered some 346,000 net hectares, of which more than 300,000 hectares are undeveloped land with considerable gas and oil exploration potential.

BG Canada's activities form an important part of BG Group's global operations, which cover four key business segments —exploration and production, liquefied natural gas, transmission and distribution, and power generation.

BG Canada's production assets are concentrated in four areas:

- Bubbles, in northeastern British Columbia (NEBC), is BG Canada's largest production asset, with 57 wells, 34 kilometers of pipelines, and four compression and dehydration facilities;

BG GROUP

- Ojay, also in NEBC, has five wells and one processing facility;
- Copton, in western Alberta, with 14 wells in the Canadian Deep Basin, has over 45 kilometers of pipelines and two processing facilities; and
- Waterton, in southwestern Alberta, has one well, in which the company holds a 50 percent interest with Shell Canada Limited.

These areas serve as a base for BG Canada's acquisition and development of further positions in the western portion of the Western Canadian Sedimentary Basin and in the Foothills area of Alberta and British Columbia. In addition, in 2005 BG Canada with its partner International Frontier Resources Corporation was awarded blocks CMV4 and CMV7 in the Northwest Territories, extending its activities into the central Mackenzie Valley.

BG Canada aims to create new opportunities within Canada's attractive exploration and production areas. The company's strategy is to continue developing the assets within its core areas, while also growing by investing in the acquisition and development of assets in new areas. It is committed to conducting all activities safely and responsibly.

In early 2006, BG Group acquired a 33.33 percent equity share in 849,840 hectares of land in the foothills area of the Alaskan North Slope, which will be managed by BG Canada.

BG Canada has a staff of approximately 100, including contractors. The company is headquartered in Calgary, Alberta, and has an office in Fort St. John, British Columbia.

Above left and right:
BG Canada Exploration and Production Inc. has assets throughout northwest Canada. The company's Bubbles facility in northeastern British Columbia is BG Canada's largest production asset.

Kinder Morgan Canada Inc.

In 2005, Kinder Morgan Inc. purchased Terasen Pipelines, which had reliably transported petroleum for half a century and which will continue to tap the vast energy resources of Alberta's oil sands while preserving the environment and supporting its communities.

Right: In 1952, just one year after being chartered, the Trans Mountain Oil Pipeline Company—the predecessor company of Kinder Morgan Canada Inc.—began the challenge of building a mainline pipe system across rugged mountains and sensitive wetlands, waterways, and parklands. Today, Kinder Morgan Canada serves many markets across North America with its 4,500-kilometre pipeline network.

Kinder Morgan Canada Inc.'s (formerly Terasen Pipelines) 4,500-kilometre pipeline network gives more than 35 Canadian and U.S. corporations choice and flexibility when moving their products to market. Its crude-oil pipeline systems span North America from the Fort McMurray oil sands of northern Alberta to the coast of British Columbia and Washington State and as far east as Illinois. The main systems—Trans Mountain, Corridor, Express-Platte, and Puget Sound—flow with crude oil, refined petroleum, aviation turbine (jet) fuel, diluted bitumen, and other products. The company's Westridge Marine Terminal in the Port of Vancouver ships crude oil overseas and stores jet fuel for the Vancouver International Airport.

Chartered in 1951 as Trans Mountain (a name that suggests the challenge it faced), the company built a mainline system across rugged mountains and sensitive wetlands, waterways, and parklands, requiring perseverance and tough-fibered pioneers to do the job. Triumphing over topography and the skepticism of naysayers, Trans Mountain completed the pipeline in just 30 months. The first oil shipment, from the Edmonton Terminal to the Burnaby Terminal in Vancouver, arrived on October 17, 1953.

Designed to transport crude oil only, the pipelines were eventually modified to let customers "batch" refined products as well (one of the world's few pipelines that can), meaning the same pipeline can flow with different products separated by density and other physical properties. In 2000 the company returned to the drawing board to build the 493-kilometre Corridor pipeline system linking the Athabasca Oil Sands Project in Fort McMurray to Shell Canada's Scotford refinery in Fort Saskatchewan, Alberta, and to marketing terminals in Edmonton. Two years and 2.5 million man-hours later, the system was completed on-time and on-budget with an outstanding safety record.

In 2003 Terasen Pipelines—now proudly operating as Kinder Morgan Canada—partnered with two Canadian investors to acquire the Express and Platte pipeline

systems from EnCana Corporation. The Express pipeline system transports light, medium, and heavy crude oil produced in western Canada from Hardisty, Alberta, to U.S. markets in Montana, Wyoming, Utah, and Colorado. The Platte system transports Canadian and Rocky Mountain products to Kansas, Illinois, and other midwestern U.S. carriers. Today Kinder Morgan Canada's continent-wide petroleum transportation business provides two major links between Canadian producers and U.S. markets.

Environmental Responsibility

Kinder Morgan Canada respects the environment. An environmental review precedes every project to identify protection measures, to inform landowners of proposed activity, and to obtain the necessary permits. Its Environmental Management System oversees all aspects of the business and upholds strict standards. Since pipelines have to weather heat, ice, rain, wind, and earthquakes, the company vigilantly treats its pipes for corrosion, tests them for pressure tolerance, monitors them with computers

that can remotely shut down pipe segments if necessary, and deploys teams to find and fix defects. Flexible and resilient, Kinder Morgan Canada's modern steel pipelines can even withstand violent earthquakes.

Community Responsibility

Communities along Kinder Morgan Canada's systems see more of the company than just its pipelines; they see a community partner. The company promotes safety, prevents hazards, makes sure that people know where its pipelines are, notifies them of maintenance and construction work, prepares them for possible emergencies, and communicates transparently in the event of a crisis.

Beyond safety and awareness, the company supports arts and education, enhances wild habitats, and participates in community events where it operates. Kinder Morgan Canada's Aboriginal Engagement Program includes indigenous people in any planning that involves aboriginal land. On a regular basis, the company shares information, listens to concerns, and

redresses the grievances of aboriginal communities. Mutual respect and trust yield cooperation.

Future Responsibility: Oil Sands

As oil demand rises and refineries find better ways to extract oil from sand, Alberta's vast oil sands— the largest in the world next to Saudi Arabia's—will change the balance of global oil production, helping supply North America and overseas markets. Kinder Morgan Canada has factored the oil sands into its expansion projects, which will accommodate an expected 2.6 million barrels per day

in 2006 and more than 3.1 million barrels per day in 2010 (up from 2.2 million barrels per day in 2005).

The Corridor and Trans Mountain expansions and the Anchor Loop will move more products at a faster rate, meeting the needs of shippers and, ultimately, consumers.

As Canada's petroleum industry grows, Kinder Morgan Canada Inc. will do its part to build and improve the country's energy infrastructure. And in doing so, it will keep people, property, and the environment its top priorities.

Above: Kinder Morgan Canada's main pipeline systems—the Corridor (shown here), the Trans Mountain, the Express-Platte, and the Puget Sound—flow with crude oil, refined petroleum, diluted bitumen, and other products that fuel Canada and the United States. With the expansion of the Corridor and Trans Mountain systems, these products will be moved at an even faster rate to meet the needs of shippers and consumers.

Western Lakota Energy Services Inc.

This preferred drilling contractor, the fifth-largest in Canada and growing, builds and uses new, safe, efficient drilling rigs to tap Alberta's oil and gas resources, while forging true partnerships with many of the province's Aboriginal communities by providing jobs and investment opportunities.

Western Lakota Energy Services Inc. is one of Canada's fastest-growing oil and gas drilling contractors. Since the company's first two drilling rigs began operating in December 2001, the fleet has grown to a count of 30 rigs. The company operates eight coal bed methane/oil sands coring/preset rigs under its subsidiary Akuna Drilling. This entity has been established as a private trust in which Western Lakota is the primary unit holder and over 30 Aboriginal communities have purchased equity. Western Lakota also operates five coil tubing units under its subsidiary Command Coil Services Inc.

Headquartered in Calgary, Western Lakota designs and constructs state-of-the-art drilling rigs in Nisku while Akuna Drilling operates out of Strathmore.

Right: Western Lakota Energy Services Inc. is headquartered in Calgary, Alberta. Shown here are Western Lakota employees at work on the drilling rig floor.

In a unique business model, 10 of the rigs are owned in separate 50–50 partnerships with five Aboriginal communities, including the Dene Tha' First Nation (five rigs), Saddle Lake First Nation (two rigs), Duncan's First Nation (one rig), Horse Lake First Nation (one rig), and the Blood Tribe (one rig). Western Lakota acts as the general partner in these partnerships, coordinating construction, marketing, finances, personnel, safety, and all other aspects associated with the day-to-day management of the drilling rigs. Collectively, the company's management team brings more than 100 years of industry experience to the job—experience that has led to early success for the young business.

"Western Lakota has achieved strong results since we began operating," said Elson McDougald, president and CEO. "In a period of only four years, we have become the fifth-largest drilling contractor in Canada due to our strong in-field performance, good safety record, customer focus, and unique Aboriginal relationships."

In 2005, the Samson Cree Nation exchanged its 50 percent ownership interest in three drilling rigs, which were partnered with Western Lakota, for shares in the company, and Chief Victor Buffalo of the Samson Cree Nation was appointed a director of Western Lakota. In early

2006, the Métis Nation of Alberta also exchanged its 100 percent ownership interest in a drilling rig, which was operated by Western Lakota, for shares in the company and trust units of its subsidiary Akuna Drilling Trust.

Western Lakota's commitment to providing investment and employment opportunities to First Nation and Métis communities sets it apart from other companies in the industry, provides access to many oil and gas customers, and generates interest from investors. Today about 20 percent of its workforce is Aboriginal, and it has an innovative training program to introduce more Aboriginal people to the energy-services industry.

The Drilling Rig Training Program is a two-week course delivered directly to those individuals in the Aboriginal community interested in entering the energy services industry. The first seven days consist of personal-empowerment training where individuals are given the opportunity to identify and address questions, concerns, or fears they may have regarding entering the workforce. The next five days involve both training on a portable drilling-rig platform, allowing students to gain hands-on skills, and also classroom instruction, where they discuss safety issues and learn the theory behind drilling rigs. The final two days encompass emergency first-aid training and hydrogen-sulfide safety training.

Students who complete the course are employed by Western Lakota when positions are available. Once fully crewed, the organization makes the trainees available for hire by other oil- and gas-related companies. Once they enter the workforce, the company's training program coordinator stays in touch with the graduates to help them work through any problems they may encounter. The program has achieved a 90 percent completion rate and an approximate 80 percent retention rate of graduates. The company has been recognized at the silver level of achievement in the Progressive Aboriginal Relations program and, in early 2005, received the Alberta Chamber of Commerce's Best Practices Award for Aboriginal Relations.

In addition, McDougald won the 2005 Prairies Entrepreneur of the Year Award for the Energy Services Sector, as well as a special citation at the Canadian Entrepreneur of the Year Awards for the company's work in Aboriginal communities.

In January 2006, *Alberta Venture* magazine ranked Western Lakota number three on its "Fast 50" list of fastest growing Alberta companies. In only four years of existence, the company's market capitalization has grown from less than $20 million to more than $750 million. By focusing on cost control and strong day rates, the company rewards its shareholders and partners with consistently solid financial performance.

The company gives back to the communities that help support it, contributing to organizations such as rural hospitals, United Way, and its Aboriginal partners' communities.

Strong relationships with its partners, shareholders, customers, suppliers, and employees are integral to Western Lakota's success. The company takes pride in its crews and their productivity, safety, and technical capabilities. Western Lakota committed to building 21 more rigs and three coil tubing service units in its 2006 Construction Program. With its high-performance crews and new-generation drilling fleet, Western Lakota is positioned for continued success.

Above right: Alberta government, Aboriginal partner, and Western Lakota representatives celebrate the launch of the company's Drilling Rig Training Program. Above center: Western Lakota employees work on one of the company's drilling rigs. Above left: Shown here is an example of Western Lakota's state-of-the-art drilling rigs.

McDaniel & Associates
Consultants Ltd.

This Calgary-based independent consulting firm is a leader in providing petroleum geology, reservoir engineering, and evaluation services to companies worldwide, supplying accurate analyses and superior, ethical services.

McDaniel & Associates Consultants Ltd. is an independent Canadian consulting firm that has been providing a wide range of evaluation services to the petroleum industry worldwide for more than 50 years. Headquartered in Calgary, with a staff of professional engineers and geologists, McDaniel consults on all aspects of petroleum geology, reservoir engineering, and reserves evaluation for private and public companies, including major financial institutions, around the world.

Formed in 1955 by Rod McDaniel, the firm has evaluated most oil and gas developments in the Western Sedimentary Basin and Canada's frontiers. Its engineers and geologists have earned the firm a reputation for superior petroleum reservoir engineering, reserve estimation, economic evaluation, geological studies, and expert-witness testimony.

When oil and gas prices fluctuate, oil and gas companies need accurate reserve estimates and cash-flow forecasts to make decisions and inform shareholders. Energy companies turn to McDaniel & Associates for such information, advice, and evaluations. Impartiality, reliability, and excellence are the values that stand McDaniel & Associates in good stead.

Clients depend on this firm's services. McDaniel & Associates has evaluation experience in Russia, the Ukraine, Kazakhstan, the United Kingdom (onshore), the North Sea, Indonesia, Australia, Africa, the Middle East, North America, South America, Cuba, and Trinidad, among others.

Overall, McDaniel & Associates is a leader in petroleum consulting—providing clients with accurate evaluations and superior, ethical service.

Willbros MSI Canada Inc.

With nearly 100 years of experience, this fully integrated company is recognized for its expertise in the fabrication, installation, and maintenance of oil pipelines, for its record of completing projects on time and within budget, and for the high calibre of its team of professionals.

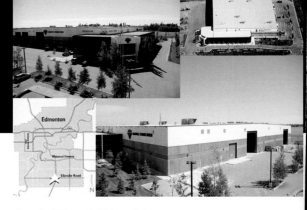

Serving a range of industry sectors in western Canada, Willbros MSI Canada Inc. is a fully integrated company that fabricates, installs, and maintains oil production facilities and pipelines. Established in 1988 in Alberta as MSI Energy Services and acquired in 2001 by Willbros Group, Inc., Willbros MSI Canada is headquartered in Edmonton, near the hub of western Canada's oil sands extraction activity.

With nearly 100 years of experience, Willbros MSI Canada's team of qualified experts in oil sands pipeline construction and maintenance ensures that projects are completed on time and within budget. The company has a long-term contract with Syncrude Canada Ltd. to maintain and construct new additions to Syncrude's tailings pipeline system at its base plant, as well as its Aurora extraction facilities. In June 2004, Willbros MSI Canada

received Syncrude's President Award for the "Most Improved Safety Program." Willbros MSI Canada also has multiyear contracts with Suncor Energy Inc. and with Albian Sands Energy Inc.

Through its 95,000-square-foot Module Fabrication and Assembly Facility in Edmonton, Willbros MSI Canada offers complete welding and fabrication services. This climate-controlled plant—one of the largest facilities of its kind in Canada—features state-of-the-art fabrication technology for the production of small and large modules for the oil field. Situated on an 18-acre yard, the facility uses leading-edge welding laboratories and techniques, thus avoiding weather-related downtime and yielding higher quality products and faster production.

Willbros MSI Canada's general fabrication facility, located in Fort McMurray, Alberta, serves clients in the Alberta energy sector. The company's field service component focuses on the maintenance of production facilities, with a growing niche market in slurry pipelines.

Overall, Willbros MSI Canada has developed leading-edge technologies to optimize production and minimize maintenance. The company's patented Expansion Barrel Puller provides a simple, cost-effective solution to dismantling slurry pipeline expansion barrels. With 200,000 pounds of thrust, the Expansion Barrel Puller also enables hydro testing and calibrating of the barrels prior to field installation. The Automated Pipeline Rotation System automatically rotates the pipes every six weeks, reducing the wear and corrosion of the pipeline.

Willbros MSI Canada's parent company, the Willbros Group, has more than 400 clients in more than 50 countries worldwide and enjoys a reputation for completing logistically difficult projects. With its expertise in pipeline construction and maintenance, and its dedication to safety and customer service, Willbros MSI Canada Inc. has become an integral part of this global operation.

Syncrude oil sand mine and refinery, Fort McMurray

Financial and Insurance Services

Profiles of Companies and Organizations

Walton International Group Inc.

Proudly headquartered in Calgary, Alberta, since 1972, the Walton International Group Inc.—renowned for 'Investing on Solid Ground'—succeeds as one of North America's most experienced land banking companies and features offices throughout Canada, the United States, and Asia.

The Alberta Centennial marks a historical moment in the evolution of Canada and serves as a monument to the entrepreneurial spirit of the province. What is known today as Walton International Group Inc., a Doherty family-owned and -operated business since 1972, is proud to be a part of Alberta's success.

'Investing on Solid Ground'

Walton is one of North America's most experienced land banking companies. Headquartered in Calgary, Alberta, Walton has offices throughout Canada, the United States, and Asia, serving more than 30,000 investors.

Walton's focus is on the purchase of strategically located raw land in the path of development of major North American cities, a concept known as land banking. Walton makes land banking, traditionally reserved for large institutions or corporations, available to individuals.

Walton brings experience and a long-standing reputation of business excellence to its clients, employees, and business partners. A foundation of traditional values in a diverse and growing economy has prefaced the creation of Walton's dynamic team. The Walton team offers expertise in the areas of real estate planning, sales, marketing, acquisitions, and business development. Walton is poised for bold, high-powered growth moving into the next centennial.

Proudly Albertan, Walton continues to invite investors from around the world to experience the "Alberta Advantage," the province's entrepreneurial edge.

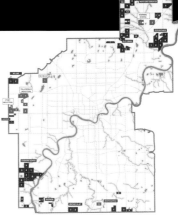

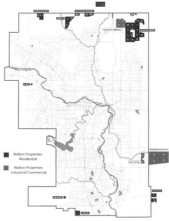

This beautiful and dynamic province offers a myriad of opportunities for realizing entrepreneurial dreams.

Mark Twain said it best: "Buy land, they're not making it anymore." The future of "Investing on Solid Ground" has never looked more promising.

A Proud History of Partnership

In 1972 Patrick J. Doherty, a native Albertan, opened a family-owned and -operated residential real estate brokerage in Calgary. The company grew to be one of the largest real estate brokerages in Alberta. Today the Walton International Group is one of North America's most experienced land banking companies, with offices in 14 cities in seven countries and over 300 full-time employees.

With its clients, Walton is now the largest land manager in the cities of Calgary and Edmonton. As a result of the "Alberta Advantage," Walton and its clients have built a solid foundation of extraordinary growth in Alberta that has now paved the way for their future success.

Walton has expanded and will continue to expand into new markets across North America. Walton's vision is to become one of the world's largest land banking companies.

Continuing to offer unique real estate structured investments to clients with professionalism and integrity will no doubt allow Walton International Group Inc. to realize its corporate goals. More importantly, it will allow Walton's clients to realize their investment goals.

Walton
International Group Inc.

www.waltoninternational.com

Above left: An aerial photograph portrays Walton's North Point Residential project in Calgary. Above right: Walton properties are highlighted on these maps of (top) Edmonton and (bottom) Calgary.

BDC

Wholly owned by the government of Canada, this financial institution—which opened its first branch in Alberta in 1956 and today has over 1,600 clients in the province—plays a complementary role in delivering financial, investment, and consulting solutions to Canadian small business.

Above left: BDC (Business Development Bank of Canada) builds close professional relationships with Canadian entrepreneurs, offering financing, investment, and consulting solutions to help them succeed in their field of business. Above right: BDC offers term financing for viable projects, including construction, with floating or fixed interest rates for terms of up to 20 years. BDC Consulting gives its customers the benefit of its extensive experience with this type of loan by referring them to qualified resources such as engineering companies, specialized notaries, building contractors, and others.

BDC is pleased to commemorate Alberta's centennial and to pay tribute to those who have helped build a great province that is a source of pride for all Canadians. Owned by the Canadian government, BDC (Business Development Bank of Canada) is a development bank that helps small and medium-sized businesses expand and compete for market share. It encourages entrepreneurship, knowing that today's fledgling companies may be the success stories of the future.

Having opened its first Alberta branch in Calgary in 1956, BDC has witnessed first hand the emergence of an increasingly diversified economy with the development of industries such as oil and gas, forestry, agribusiness, nanotechnology, and medical research. It has seen that as a result of hard work and vision, Alberta has become a powerhouse of the Canadian economy. BDC supported the province's entrepreneurs from the beginning, and its commitment has remained unaltered to this day.

Over the years, BDC has strengthened its presence in Alberta. To better serve the needs of Alberta's entrepreneurs and reinforce its commitment to the economic development of the province, BDC has a network of eight branches in Alberta and two Entrepreneurship Centers located in Calgary and Edmonton. The mission of these centers is to offer smaller businesses customized solutions, including financing and consulting advice, to help them become more competitive in their target markets.

From 1995 to 2005 alone, the number of BDC clients in Alberta grew from 950 to 1,636, a 72 percent increase. As a result, in the same period BDC's lending commitment to Alberta businesses rose exponentially by 195 percent, from $186 million to $548 million.

The importance of BDC's role as a development bank goes beyond these figures. BDC supports a wide array of business categories in Alberta; construction, manufacturing, retail, and fast-growing industry sectors represent key targets for its support. Knowledge-based and business-service industries also benefit from BDC's business solutions and are thriving in Alberta.

BDC's seasoned and dedicated professionals serve the business needs of a growing number of clients. These

entrepreneurs represent Canada's main industry sectors, including tourism, and innovative businesses in the new economy, including information technology, telecommunications, and biotechnology.

BDC has gone the extra mile in Alberta to ensure that its services provide added value for its clients. In a larger perspective, BDC has consistently fulfilled its mandate of supporting the creation and development of Canadian small and medium-sized

businesses with innovative and customized business solutions in the form of loans, venture capital investments, subordinate financing, and consulting services. BDC considers its commitment to such support to be of utmost importance since small and medium-sized businesses account for more than 40 percent of the Canadian economy and employ two-thirds of the country's working population.

Although the business environment has changed significantly over time,

BDC constantly succeeds in establishing enduring business relationships with its clients by responding to their timely requirements and by extending its reach in all regions of the country, including Alberta.

"Client connection" is one of BDC's most cherished core values. In fact, BDC's customer focus follows that of its business solutions: growing over the long term. Throughout the years, BDC has never lost sight of its primary objective: building and

maintaining close business relationships with each and every one of its clients. BDC is especially proud to help entrepreneurs—in Alberta and elsewhere in Canada—achieve their business objectives so they can in turn contribute to the development of a strong national economy.

TSX Venture Exchange

Canada's public venture capital stock market brings investors together with emerging innovative companies that are building Alberta's future.

recognition for their leadership in providing equity finance for mining and oil and gas companies.

In 2004, TSX Group expanded its Calgary presence by acquiring Natural Gas Exchange (NGX), which trades natural gas and electricity in Canada and the United States.

Less well known are the capital market innovations that Alberta pioneered and that TSX Venture Exchange now brings to entrepreneurs and investors across Canada.

TSX Venture's Capital Pool Company® (CPC) program evolved from a listing technique that was introduced in Alberta almost 20 years ago. CPCs bring emerging companies that need capital together with experienced public company operators. The CPC innovation is now the most popular method for going public on the Exchange.

TSX Venture is Canada's first national stock exchange for emerging growth companies and it is also the world's oldest venture exchange that helps micro- and small-capitalization companies raise capital. Canada has developed stock exchanges that operate so efficiently that even start-ups with modest financial resources are able to access public equity capital. In that, it is unique in the world.

While stock exchanges exist elsewhere for small companies, none has listing, disclosure, and governance standards comparable to TSX Venture's.

The Exchange believes that its standards, reinforced by TSX Group's reputation for quality and integrity, play an important role in its success and also in the achievements of its listed companies.

TSX Group is proud of Alberta's leadership in the public venture capital market, and TSX Venture Exchange looks forward with confidence to its future in Calgary.

TSX Venture Exchange's roots run deep in Alberta. One of its predecessor markets, the Calgary Stock Exchange, was founded to help finance Alberta's first oil discoveries.

The Exchange was incorporated in 1913, a year after drilling began in Turner Valley and more than 25 years before Leduc Number One came in. Alberta's oil boom had started, and TSX Venture Exchange was there.

Regional stock exchanges around the world began consolidating in the late 1990s, and Toronto Stock Exchange (TSX) joined forces with the Alberta exchange in 2001. The following year, TSX Group, TSX Venture Exchange's corporate parent, was the first North American stock exchange operator to become a publicly traded company.

Soon, TSX and TSX Venture began working together to gain international

Above: TSX VentureExchange has a long history of funding natural resource exploration. Now financing is also available on the Exchange for technology, biotech, and industrial companies.

		137,000	13
		140,000	13
		89,678	13
		117,451	13
		74,637	13
		70,400	13
	47,115	84,015	13
		104,891	13
		61,777	13

Health Care, Pharmaceuticals, and Biotechnology

Profiles of Companies and Organizations

Gimbel Eye Centre

This world-renowned eye clinic and its expert associates—guided by Dr. Howard V. Gimbel—restore or enhance the vision of local and international patients, teach the present and next generation of ophthalmology specialists, and expand the frontiers of ophthalmological knowledge and surgical skills.

Right: Dr. Howard V. Gimbel, born and raised on a farm near Beiseker, Alberta, devotes himself to eye health and to transmitting his wisdom and experience to other doctors. Far right: The Gimbel Eye Centres in Calgary and Edmonton each encompass two operating rooms and a laser surgery suite, where Dr. Gimbel and his associates have performed more than 170,000 surgeries since 1964.

Purpose, vision, and values have been the hallmarks of Dr. Howard V. Gimbel's world-renowned ophthalmology practice in Alberta since 1964.

Dr. Gimbel's excellence—and that of the doctors he handpicks as associates for his Calgary and Edmonton Centres—has impacted more than 350,000 patients from more than 50 countries, and has made Alberta a destination for quality eye care.

Born and raised on a farm near Beiseker, Alberta, Dr. Gimbel is motivated by a deep passion to impact people's lives by restoring or enhancing their vision as well as a willingness to share his experiences with other doctors. Surgeons from all over the world come to visit the Gimbel Eye Centre to learn from Dr. Gimbel firsthand. Many attend for one-year fellowship training to advance their specialization and to observe and learn from the techniques and practices of Dr. Gimbel and his team of excellent associates. By invitation, Dr. Gimbel has frequently broadcast live surgeries via satellite to major ophthalmology conferences around the globe in order to assist in advancing the skills of other eye surgeons.

At great effort and expense, Dr. Gimbel has also personally organized and hosted international ophthalmology conferences held in Banff, Alberta. His conferences have drawn renowned faculty and attendees from around the world.

After more than four decades of innovative surgery, teaching, and the development of numerous new techniques, Dr. Gimbel is frequently honoured and recognized for his contributions to the world of ophthalmology. Of particular note, in 1992 he received the Alberta Order of Excellence in recognition of service of the greatest distinction and of singular excellence. In 1996 his ophthalmology peers voted him one of the top ophthalmologists in the world. And in 2005 Dr. Gimbel was bestowed with a Lifetime Achievement award by his Canadian colleagues.

Dr. Gimbel's willingness and his unselfish sharing of his innovation have been a source of inspiration and advancement that has made a difference in people's lives and in the international profession of ophthalmology.

For more than 40 years, the Gimbel Eye Centre has stood for creating momentum in ophthalmology as patients and professionals from around the world have sought out the Alberta-grown expertise in cataract and refractive surgery that is available at this eye clinic.

The legacy of innovative excellence supports a firm foundation for future endeavours and for continuing service with competence, convenience, and compassion at the Gimbel Eye Centre.

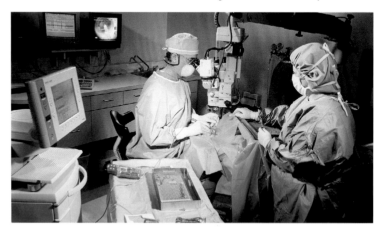

Banner Pharmacaps Inc.

This global leader in researching, developing, and producing innovative pharmaceutical oral dosage softgels and nutritional supplements for the health care industry, delivers products to its Canadian customers from a state-of-the-art containment facility in Olds, Alberta.

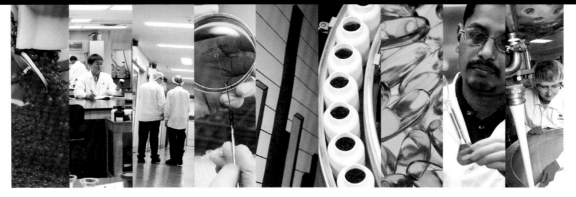

Banner Pharmacaps Inc.—an innovative leader in manufacturing encapsulated pharmaceutical and nutritional products—draws on 130 years of collective experience to provide consumers with softgel medications that are better tasting, easier to swallow and digest, and more fully absorbed into the bloodstream. Committed to meeting the needs of the marketplace, Banner has created new softgel variants that offer advantages over other dosage forms, enabling the company to place itself at the forefront of patented dosage-form technology.

From its headquarters in High Point, North Carolina, Banner employs a team of Ph.D.s and scientists who develop the most effective drug-delivery technologies available. With experience in biochemistry, cell biology, pharmaceutics, industrial pharmacy, and analytical chemistry, these research and development experts focus on combining technologies to enhance softgel drug delivery. Topping the list of Banner's breakthrough technologies are EnteriCare™ enteric softgels, Chewels™ chewable gels, EcoCaps™ non-animal

softgels, Soflet® Gelcaps, and Versatrol™ controlled-release softgels.

Banner's over-the-counter product line ranges from gastrointestinal products to cough and cold products. In its Mexico plant, Banner manufactures suppositories for both branded and private-label products. The company supplies its Soflet Gelcaps to major pharmaceutical firms and private-label suppliers for analgesics and feminine pain relievers. Soflet Gelcaps are also being promoted as a deterrent to drug product counterfeiting. Banner supplies the nutrition market with dosage forms for vitamin E, fish oil, and CoQ10, and collaborates with the product

development teams of nutrition companies to develop custom products.

Banner Pharmacaps Canada, located in Olds, includes two facilities that meet all requirements of current Good Manufacturing Practices and have been inspected and approved by Health Canada and the U.S. Food and Drug Administration. Standardized operating and quality control procedures, detailed record keeping, and strict sanitary measures are consistent throughout this manufacturing and containment facility.

The company's worldwide production sites are located in Alberta, Canada; High Point, North Carolina; Mexico

City, Mexico; Tilburg, The Netherlands; and Bangalore and Gujarat, India.

From the first stages of research and development to the last stages of sophisticated production, every product Banner makes is customized to the client's specifications and made in state-of-the-art plants that conform to the company's high standards of excellence and care. Whether it is selecting the right dosage form or working with complex formulas to enhance bioavailability, Banner Pharmacaps Inc. remains committed to partnering with nutritional and pharmaceutical companies to ensure that the best products reach the consumer.

Above, all images:
The bottom line for
Banner Pharmacaps Inc.
is health—a healthy
business, healthy partnerships, and, most of all,
healthy people.

Information Technology and Telecommunications

Profiles of Companies and Organizations

Apex AVSI
(Audio Visual Systems Integration)

Bringing Canadians together in efficient, productive, and memorable ways is the power behind this leading audiovisual integrator, which provides best-in-class presentation products, systems integration, and videoconferencing services to the business, education, government, and retail markets.

APEX AVSI
AUDIO VISUAL SYSTEMS INTEGRATION

Above: Headquartered in Calgary with branch locations in Edmonton, Lethbridge, Vancouver, Toronto, and London, Apex AVSI has created effective, powerful presentation environments across Canada, from small meeting rooms to grand boardrooms, from classrooms to lecture halls, from retail stores to international airports.

Apex AVSI (Audio Visual Systems Integration) company president Jeff Faber pinpoints the moment that transformed his company. "We were making a presentation to a Fortune 500 company in the mid 1980s. The sales team and I prepared a solid product pitch that we presented to the company's CEO and his team about the integration solution we were proposing."

Faber recalls that, when the demonstration was over, the CEO looked up and complimented the team on the presentation. "He told us that our solution was impressive and certainly performed better than other products they reviewed. But what he was really after

had nothing to do with simple product specs at all," Faber says. The CEO said he was looking for a broader solution, something that would make their company more productive and efficient. "It was a major setback," Faber says. "But we went back to the drawing board and six months later sold them their first integrated audiovisual system. Since that day, they have remained our client for the past 20 years."

Faber and the Apex AVSI team spend their time working with a wide range of clients and applications, not just the boards of Fortune 500 companies. Their client list includes education institutions and schools, major corporations, training facilities, government agencies, and small businesses. The company has earned many accolades and designations over the years, including the exclusive Canadian ranking among audiovisual integrators of Gold Certified AudioVisual Solutions Provider from InfoComm International.

Tim St. Louis, partner and vice president of sales, says the market for

audiovisual systems has expanded and customers are more critical than ever when choosing the right system. "Today's customer is well informed on the availability and functionality of audiovisual products. They know which projectors, interactive whiteboards, and data conferencing products are out there in the marketplace. It is our job to build the model from these pieces of presentation technology to form a tool that best reflects the communication goals of their organization," St. Louis says.

A case in point is Southern Alberta Institute of Technology (SAIT). Apex AVSI has worked with SAIT since 1998 on scoping the right configuration of technology. Guy Mallabone, SAIT vice president of external relations, says SAIT is proud of its relationship with Apex AVSI. "As Canada's leading polytechnic educational institution, SAIT is proud to work with other partners who are leaders in their field. Apex AVSI is clearly one of these partners, and we welcome their innovative and creative approach to working on tomorrow's challenges today."

Apex AVSI services clients from six branch locations across Canada. Since its inception in 1980, the company has been strategically aligned with numerous manufacturers, including NEC Visual Systems, Toshiba Canada, and Smart Technologies. "NEC is extremely fortunate to have Apex AVSI sell and service our projector and plasma product lines in Canada," says Pierre Richer, senior vice president, NEC Visual Divisions, Americas. "The knowledge and support of the Apex AVSI team is critical to customer satisfaction when using NEC products. It's one of the many reasons they have become our largest partner in Canada."

Bringing workforces or students together in meaningful ways is a tall order for any communications company. But Faber, St. Louis, and the team at Apex AVSI seem to be getting the formula right. It is one practiced by other successful businesses: Listen to the customer, deliver value and benefits, and have a grasp of the bigger picture. For more information, visit the company's Web site at apexavsi.com or call 403-255-4123.

Manufacturing

Profiles of Companies and Organizations

Korite International

Operating in Calgary since 1979, Korite International—the premier miner and manufacturer of Alberta's rare and exotic gem, ammolite—produces some 90 percent of the world's supply of the rarest precious stone in existence.

For 27 years, the founders of Korite International have persevered to transform ammolite's reputation from that of a little-known iridescent fossil to an internationally recognized and highly sought after gem.

Ammolite—The Sleeping Beauty of the Gem World

As rare as they are beautiful, all ammolite gems are one of a kind—unique in brilliance, colour, and pattern.

Ammolite is formed from an ancient marine fossil deposit called ammonite. Although sources of ammonite exist in other locations around the globe, it is only in one isolated region of southern Alberta that this deposit produces the gemstone ammolite. The vibrant colors seen only in ammolite are the effect of 70 million years of tectonic pressure and resulting heat as well as mineralization from surrounding soils. A true geological wonder, ammolite is one of nature's rarest gems.

It is predicted that the world's supply of high grade ammolite will be exhausted within 15 years (*Gems & Gemology*, Geological Institute of America, spring 2001). Due to increasing demand and limited supply, the highest grades of ammolite have increased in price by 10 percent to 20 percent per year for the last decade.

The chemical composition of ammolite is aragonite, the same mineral that composes the exotic South Sea pearl. This places ammolite in the same family as pearls, and places ammolite as the most rare and brilliant of this family. Like pearls, ammolite has a natural hardness of 4.0 to 4.5 (on the Mohs scale).

Through years of research and development, Korite has mastered specialized cutting techniques which have increased ammolite's durability to that of sapphire's 8.5, enabling Korite to offer a lifetime guarantee.

People treasure ammolite for its brilliance and amazing play of colour. This unique gemstone is prized throughout the world, especially in Europe, Asia, and North America for the health and environmental benefits it is believed to bring. Feng shui masters and health practitioners recommend ammolite for its natural positive energy to promote health, wealth, and enlightenment.

From the fossil-rich terrain where ammolite is unearthed, Korite occasionally uncovers complete ammonite specimens. These exceptionally rare iridescent fossils are cherished by collectors and exhibited by the world's most renowned museums. Working closely with the Royal Tyrrell Museum in Drumheller, Alberta, Korite is credited with significant scientific discoveries in paleontology.

Korite—Quality, Exclusivity, and Elegance

Korite International is the ammolite supplier to the world. Registered in 1981 as an official gemstone, ammolite has attained the level of recognition it deserves as a result of the dedication and determination of the Korite founders.

It took years of exploration and test mining before Korite discovered the world's first commercially viable ammolite deposit and developed the intensive mining process still in use today.

Korite operates heavy machinery to remove up to 25 metres of surface rock to reach the highest quality and most productive ammolite gem material. Painstaking effort is put forth as every handful of earth is searched for gem material; any full fossils found are set aside for restoration. Over the years, Korite has excavated 16 hectares of land, 12 of which have been completely restored to their natural state. Korite has proudly set new environmental standards in its reclamation process.

Once the ammolite gem rough has been recovered and sorted, it is transported to Calgary, where the gem cutting and jewellery manufacturing operations are located. In addition to its own extensive jewellery line, Korite often commissions local Albertan designers to create remarkable designs with the collection-quality ammolite gems. These award-winning designs are pictured in notable jewellery publications and can been seen in documentaries such as *Ammolite: The Birth of a Gem,* shown on the Discovery Channel in 2003.

A Brilliant Future

Ammolite is Canada's gemstone and the rare treasure of Alberta. Ammolite jewellery by Korite International is a treasured souvenir and gift item for visitors to all parts of Canada, and the impact of ammolite on the Canadian tourism sector is monumental. Originally marketed to Japanese tourists visiting the Rockies, Korite ammolite is now available in every major tourist destination across Canada and is highly sought after by visitors from around the world.

Korite ammolite is now a force in the global luxury brand marketplace.

Widespread and growing awareness throughout North America, Asia, and Europe is resulting in fierce demand and ever-increasing value of Korite ammolite.

Korite ammolite, the rare and exotic gem found only in Alberta, brings the beauty of this region to tourist centers worldwide. Awareness and appreciation for Alberta's gem will continue to grow as Korite ammolite is discovered by jewellery connoisseurs around the world.

Rare, precious, and highly sought after, ammolite is a true Alberta gem. With vision and passion, Korite International has built a strong reputation for ammolite and a treasured legacy for Albertans.

KORITE
AMMOLITE
WWW.KORITE.COM

This page, above: Heavy machinery is used to mine ammolite, which occurs in strata lying between 15 and 65 metres below the surface. Korite International refills areas once deposits are exhausted. Opposite page, left: Ammolite gemstones can display all colours of the spectrum, though red and green are the most common. Opposite page, right: Ammolite, the rarest of the three biogenic gems— the other two being pearl and amber—is derived from fossilized ammonites such as this magnificent specimen from the Upper Cretaceous epoch.

Reimer International Inc.

Durable and designed for ease and efficiency, this Alberta company's mobile concrete mixers—which do the job of both a batch plant and conventional cement truck—save concrete businesses time, trouble, money, and material, and they suit projects from patios to oil-field cementing.

Above: The Reimer Mobile Volumetric Concrete Mixer is designed for durability, reliability, and ease of operation. Every component of the mixer meets Reimer International Inc.'s high performance standards, from its wireless remote control to its state-of-the-art hydraulic system.

Reimer International Inc. began 63 years ago when Walter Reimer moved to the small Alberta town of Didsbury and started General Trucking. Walter served the community by hauling coal, lumber, grain, livestock, sand, gravel, and general freight. He later hauled milk to Red Deer and Calgary. In 1965, he and his youngest son, Gordie, imported the first two concrete mobile mixers to Canada, from Lancaster, Pennsylvania.

These machines made concrete without using batch plants or trucks with rotating drum mixers—an innovation at the time. Cement, sand, stone, and water were loaded in four separate compartments and mixed in the truck to make fresh, ready-to-pour concrete. Local people supported the idea, and soon the little company won contracts in remote places that had no concrete supply.

Gordie Reimer began building his own mobile mixers to meet the growing demand for them. By 1995, the company (then known as Reimer Concrete Industries) ran 16 mobile mixers in four Alberta locations as well as a U.S. operation. The division Reimer International Inc. was formed in 1995 to build mobile mixers exclusively. The active concrete company was sold, and Gordie Reimer focused on manufacturing and marketing the Reimer Mobile Mixer. What began as a project to build one mixer per month has grown into a thriving company building three mixers per week.

Reimer International Mixers appear in nine of Canada's 10 provinces and all three northern territories. These mixers are also being used in 30 states south of the border, and over 100 Reimer Mixers operate daily in England. Reimer Mixers are also found in 30 countries worldwide.

Marketing Manager Steve Fillmore says, "Our goal is not only to satisfy our current customers but to introduce our machine to at least two new countries every year." The Internet (www.reimermix.com) and personal contact from Fillmore and Reimer help accomplish this.

Allan Spreeman oversees the designers, production team, and quality control to ensure a superior product. Joanne Peters, office manager, coordinates shipping, accounting, customer service, and whatever else comes through the office.

In 2005, Reimer International opened an assembly and installation plant in Greensboro, North Carolina. Currently the only Canadian manufacturer of mobile concrete mixers, Reimer International sells four models of its mixer and builds custom units as well. Reimer's mixers have worked on many projects:

- rapid set on California highways;
- diamond mine in northern Canada;
- flowable fill in Boston, Massachusetts;
- swimming pools in Florida;
- range construction in Canada and the United States;
- airport projects in Canada, the United States, and South Africa;
- foundation piles in Calgary, British Columbia (Vancouver), Montana, Florida, Hawaii, the United Kingdom, France, and South Africa;
- general construction—foundations, driveways, patios, curbs, sidewalks, and warehouses all over the world.

Satisfied customers from around the world will attest to the fact that Reimer produces a mixer that looks good, lasts a long time, and offers one of the best values on the market today.

Pratt & Whitney Canada Corporation

The number one research and development investor in Canada's aerospace sector, this company is a leader in making and maintaining airplane and helicopter engines for aircraft manufacturers worldwide, with a commitment to discovering advanced power solutions for its customers.

According to the Pratt & Whitney Canada Corporation (P&WC), every two seconds an aircraft powered by one of its engines takes off and lands somewhere in the world. This is not surprising, considering that since 1928 the company has delivered some 60,000 engines to customers in more than 190 countries. P&WC was started by Montreal businessman James Young as a service centre for Pratt & Whitney engines built in the United States and operating in Canada. Today, P&WC is a world leader in aviation engines that power business aircraft, general aviation and regional aircraft, and helicopters. This company—which is renowned for its innovation, technical excellence, and dependability—also offers auxiliary power units and industrial gas turbines.

P&WC has an assembly and test facility in Lethbridge, Alberta. It also operates research and development, assembly, and test facilities in Mississauga, Ontario; a manufacturing installation in Halifax,

Nova Scotia; manufacturing, assembly, test, repair, and state-of-the-art research and development operations in Longueuil, near Montreal, Quebec, where the company is headquartered; and service centres around the globe. P&WC is a subsidiary of the United Technologies Corporation (UTC).

Since opening in 1993, the Lethbridge facility has become an important part of the company's global operations. The plant makes the PT6 model engines, low- and high-power turboprops, and the Twin Pacs turboshaft engines that are ordered by customers in nine countries. A number of milestones further demonstrate the efficiency and success of the Lethbridge operation. From 2003 to 2005, the staff was increased by 50 percent; the number of engines produced was doubled; and 11 years of production without a lost-time incident was achieved, setting a record among all UTC companies.

In addition, the Lethbridge facility was the winner of two prestigious

P&WC Environmental Health & Safety awards in 2003 for "Continuous Improvement and Environment" and for "Stakeholder Outreach." In 2004, the Lethbridge facility received an award for its water-quality initiatives from the Southern Alberta Environmental Group.

Over the years, P&WC has built on the legacy of the original PT6 engine. Today, it builds nine types of engines, including the PT6 turbo-prop/turboshaft; the JT15D turbofan; the PW100 and PW150 turboprops; the PW200 turboshaft; the PW300, PW500, and PW600 turbofans; and the PW900 auxiliary power unit. Continually advancing its methodology, tools, and approach to building engines, the company meets the needs of its customers while maintaining its position as the largest research-and-development investor in the Canadian aerospace sector.

P&WC employs 7,000 workers in Canada and about 10,000 globally. International facilities are located in

Australia, Brazil, Poland, Russia, Singapore, South Africa, the United Kingdom, and the United States, with joint ventures in China and Germany. This extensive worldwide network of service and support helps ensure that every Pratt & Whitney Canada engine upholds the company's tradition of reliability.

Above: This Pratt & Whitney Canada facility is located in Lethbridge, Alberta.

Professional and Business Services
Profiles of Companies and Organizations

Lethbridge Chamber of Commerce

'Yesterday, today, and tomorrow': for over a century, the Lethbridge Chamber of Commerce has voiced the interests of business and championed free enterprise, contributing the time, drive, and imagination of its members to the prosperity of the city.

Above left: In the early 20th century, trains crossed the 1.6-kilometre High Level Bridge, spanning the Oldman River, to ship coal from Lethbridge across Canada. Above right: The Lethbridge Chamber of Commerce, on Sixth Street downtown, began in 1889.

Lethbridge's best-known landmark is its High Level Bridge. Ever since steelworkers riveted the last bolt to it in 1909, this engineering marvel has enabled the town to grow and prosper. Predating the bridge, though, is a civic marvel even more crucial to the prosperity of Lethbridge: the Lethbridge Chamber of Commerce. Originally the Lethbridge Board of Trade and Civic Committee when it formed in 1889, the community-driven chamber has started or spearheaded almost every noteworthy civic endeavour for more than 100 years. First, the group incorporated Lethbridge as a civic entity, the Town of Lethbridge, in 1891. That done, the organization undertook other projects: creating water-sharing agreements with Montana, addressing postal concerns, building better roads and bridges, promoting and hosting the first Chautauqua (travelling tent show) in western Canada, bringing entertainment to the culturally starved prairies, and helping reopen the U.S. border to Canadian beef in 1952, along with many more projects that bettered the community.

Still a volunteer, community-driven organization, the Lethbridge Chamber of Commerce continues to advocate positive change. It helped Lethbridge recover its Airport of Entry status, an important trade advantage since no other metropolitan area in Alberta is closer to the United States. Today's list of initiatives echoes the past's; water, roads, and the United States banning Canadian beef are recurring themes. The Lethbridge Chamber continues to forge alliances and vigorously lobby municipal, provincial, and federal decision makers for needed change. Like the famous bridge that connected the town to all of Canada, the Lethbridge Chamber of Commerce connects the city to more prosperity and the promise of future growth.

execuserv plus inc.

Delivering a training program for Albertans who are unemployed and wish to start businesses of their own, this company facilitates access to program funding and provides experienced instructors and a positive setting for business coaching, building confident entrepreneurs and offering ongoing support.

Everyone in Lethbridge knows her, or has heard of her. When you mention her name, most people have either enjoyed the experience of hearing her as a motivational speaker, have been thankful for her expertise as a business consultant, have appreciated the direction they received from her thorough entrepreneurial training, or have seen her share her knowledge while contributing her time as a volunteer. This is Gillian Nish, a Lethbridge entrepreneur who is the owner of execuserv plus inc.

A New Start

People say that the population of Alberta is made up of risk takers. Nish is one of these. In 1988, she took the risk of leaving the security, prestige, and high profile of her work in the Alberta tourism industry and moved to Lethbridge to start a home-based management consulting business. The move paid off, and the business grew.

Moving Ahead

As is the case for most entrepreneurs, Nish was not content to sit back

and reap the rewards of running a successful business; she decided to expand. After 11 years of operating her home-based company, she took the broader risk of submitting a proposal to Alberta Human Resources and Employment to facilitate a self-employment program. Competition for the contract was high, and securing it would mean moving her business from its home base to a large, storefront space, as well as hiring and managing a staff, while also taking on large financial obligations. Nonetheless Nish pressed forward. She won the contract and

in fact, later won two more such contracts.

Management Consulting and Training

Today, in addition to delivering a dynamic self-employment program for the residents of Lethbridge and the surrounding region, Nish and her dedicated team of professionals offer management consulting and training for clients in the areas of tourism, small business, and the nonprofit sector and also provide strategic business planning and feasibility studies, as well as market analysis and needs-assessment studies. Additional

information about execuserv plus inc. is available by phone (403-320-5604; or, toll free, 866-669-5604).

Most Albertans are the type of people who are committed to their province and community and who get up each day and do what is needed—without bragging, complaining, or seeking recognition; they simply "do." Nish is one of these "doers." She may or may not fully appreciate the positive impact that her mentoring, counselling, and volunteering have on other people—but the people who know her do.

Testimonials

Excerpts from comments by recipients of execuserv plus training describe a range of beneficial results:

"I found the modules on the financial side of business to be really helpful, giving me a good understanding of what makes the business tick. I highly recommend this course to anyone interested in starting up a business of their own."
—Keith Ginter, *Web Development Industry*

"I have entered into a business partnership and the skills I received at execuserv plus enabled me to be a well-informed and equal partner from the very beginning of the relationship. In the past, I had always said that I never wanted to own my own business, but now that I have 'crossed over' I would never go back."
—Stephanie Hazelwood, *Orthotic Services Industry*

"I have held positions in my career that denoted higher levels of management, but that is only scratching the surface of being a small business owner. Through my execuserv plus training I was directed in the art of blending my existing skills and matching the needs of potential clients. The service was invaluable."
—Gwen Tietz, *Bookkeeping Industry*

The Medicine Hat & District Chamber of Commerce and Tourism Medicine Hat

As the 'Voice of Business' in Medicine Hat and its environs, this nonprofit organization advocates the economic growth and pro-business reform that lead to a healthy diverse community.

Above center: The Medicine Hat & District Chamber of Commerce is dedicated to business advocacy and economic development for a healthy business environment in Medicine Hat. Above right: Tourism Medicine Hat operates this Visitor Centre on the Trans-Canada Highway.

The more than 700 businesses that compose the nonprofit Medicine Hat & District Chamber of Commerce have a potent say in local, provincial, and federal government. Of Alberta's 127 chambers of commerce, the Medicine Hat chamber ranks sixth in membership, and its annual membership dues are among the lowest in the province. With all the benefits that the chamber offers, membership easily pays for itself.

In addition to the advantages of networking and education available to members through the chamber's Business Builder events, the organization offers many other benefits designed to help businesses expand their client base. It publishes the *Chamber Business Magazine* 10 times per year, which is distributed to every business in and around Medicine Hat, and members receive the *Chamber Chatter* newsletter monthly. The chamber also provides a Web site (www.medicinehatchamber.com) with full information. A chamber member's benefits include free profiles in the magazine and newsletter, a free business listing on the chamber's Web site, discounts on advertising through various media sources, free use of the chamber's boardroom, a business referral program, and access to the chamber seal for use in exporting goods, plus the opportunity to enroll in the Chambers of Commerce Group Insurance Plan, Canada's largest group benefits plan for small businesses employing from one to 50 people.

Tourism Medicine Hat invites people to enjoy the city and the region's attractions and operates the local Visitor Centre on the Trans-Canada Highway. The organization provides information on its Web site (www.tourismmedicinehat.com). Residents and tourism industry operators help make tourists' visits enjoyable, relaxing, and memorable. Among its many points of interest, the region features tours of Medicine Hat Clay Industries National Historic District's Medalta Potteries and Hycroft China factory complexes, as well as the opportunity to stand under the World's Tallest Tepee, which is 20 stories high. As Canada's sunniest city, Medicine Hat offers fine weather for vacationers to enjoy golfing, sliding down the largest outdoor waterslide in western Canada, taking a jet boat tour on the majestic South Saskatchewan River, which flows through the region, or relaxing in one of the area's beautiful parks.

Geographically, Medicine Hat is the first city in Alberta on the Trans-Canada Highway and the Canadian Pacific Railway, which gives local businesses a major advantage. The industries of Medicine Hat rival those of Canada's most modern industrialized cities. And the Medicine Hat & District Chamber of Commerce helps businesses flourish.

City Hall, Medicine Hat

The Calgary Chamber of Commerce

As the primary voice of business in Calgary, The Calgary Chamber of Commerce partners with the corporate community to promote and support business and provides valuable networking opportunities for its 3,500 members.

One of Canada's most respected business organizations, The Calgary Chamber of Commerce empowers companies to grow and succeed by advocating lower taxes, fewer regulations, fiscal wisdom, and networking among businesspeople.

With 3,500 members, The Chamber is Calgary's most influential and resourceful business advocate. It holds instructive seminars, gives member-to-member discounts, organizes networking events, and hosts guest speakers. In all,

Right: This historic 1912 building in downtown Calgary, owned and occupied by The Calgary Chamber of Commerce, provides a full-service business centre for members.

The Calgary Chamber of Commerce hosts about 130 events per year.

One annual event, Small Business Week Expo, celebrates Alberta's entrepreneurial spirit. The event, cosponsored by Mount Royal College and BDC (the Business Development Bank of Canada), lets entrepreneurs network and share ideas at conferences, workshops, trade fairs, luncheons, and other events. Closing with an awards dinner, Small Business Week Expo honors the RBC Royal Bank Small Business of the Year and the Bennett Jones Emerging Enterprise of the Year.

The Chamber was formed in 1891 as the Calgary Board of Trade to "advance commercial, industrial, and civic interests and promote integrity and good faith in business." The board upheld trade ethics and ensured fair labour conditions. Renamed The Calgary Chamber of Commerce in 1950, it helped the city grow into a major commercial centre by adhering to its simple mission: lead and serve

the Calgary business community, valuing its diversity.

The Calgary Chamber of Commerce is the second-largest in Canada. The 1912 building it owns and occupies, a former Odd Fellow temple, is today a modern, full-service business centre with fine dining, day offices, a wireless hotspot, meeting rooms, boardrooms, a café, and more—all under one roof in the middle of downtown Calgary and all at the disposal of Chamber members.

The Calgary Chamber of Commerce is an active member of the Alberta Chambers of Commerce—a collection of 127 chambers—and the Canadian Chamber of Commerce, with more than 850 chambers of commerce among its membership. This participation gives The Calgary Chamber of Commerce greater strength and increases its ability to influence all levels of government. Its future plans include developing new products and services, promoting itself through increased visibility and public relations, and maintaining its position as an influential business advocate.

SADDLEDOME

Pengrowth Saddledome, Calgary

Edmonton Chamber of Commerce

With a legacy more than a century in the making, this organization strives to create the best environment for the businesses of Edmonton to flourish and grow, providing numerous networking events, affinity and discount programs, and information referrals and advocating at all levels of government on behalf of its members.

Above: The Edmonton Chamber of Commerce is based at the World Trade Centre Edmonton (WTCE), which it owns and operates. The building is located at 9990 Jasper Avenue in Edmonton, Alberta. Visitors from around the world are welcomed at the WTCE, where numerous service facilities are available, including meeting and conference facilities, an information centre, an airport passenger shuttle, and a restaurant.

Legacy—the word conveys strength and stability. It speaks of time-honoured traditions and longevity. As the Edmonton Chamber of Commerce celebrated the 100-year legacy of its province in 2005, it also celebrated the pioneering entrepreneurs who literally built Alberta's foundations, contributed to its economy, and overcame adversity to pave the way for the prosperity society enjoys today.

Exponential Growth

In 1889, a group of 33 Edmonton businesspersons signed the required certificate of formation to launch the first Edmonton Chamber of Commerce (called the Edmonton Board of Trade until 1928). Since then, the organization has seen exponential growth and met change head on to become one of the largest chambers of commerce in Canada. With more than 2,700 members, in every facet of industry, large and small, the Edmonton Chamber of Commerce continually works to create the best environment possible for business in Alberta's capital city.

Providing Support

As "the official voice of business in the Edmonton area," the Edmonton Chamber of Commerce acts as an advocate for its members by contributing to public policy and debate at the municipal level. Through its affiliations with the Alberta Chambers of Commerce and the Canadian Chamber of Commerce, it works to influence both provincial and federal government decision makers to benefit its members. It provides additional information on its Web site (www.edmontonchamber.com).

The Edmonton Chamber of Commerce creates value for its members by hosting more than 140 networking events per year, offering a host of affinity and discount programs and responding to business inquiries with referrals for programs and services.

Access to World Trade

The Edmonton Chamber of Commerce also provides access to international markets through the World Trade Centre Edmonton (WTCE). A member of the World Trade Centers Association, the WTCE represents some 277 member organizations in 75 countries. It is the only such centre located between Toronto in eastern Canada and Vancouver on the west coast.

A Hub of Business Activity

The WTCE building, owned and operated by the Edmonton Chamber of Commerce, is a "home away from home" for businesses. Welcoming visitors from Edmonton and around the world, it is a hub of activity. The building is also home to an array of diverse business interests and services.

The WTCE building provides headquarters for the Edmonton Chamber of Commerce, and among its other tenants are Edmonton Economic Development Corporation and Edmonton Tourism. The Downtown Visitor Information Centre is on the main floor, as are Airport Express air passenger services and the depot for Sky Shuttle transport to Edmonton International Airport. Other tenants include Ruth's Chris Steak House, a world-class restaurant facility, and Junior Achievement of Northern Alberta & the Northwest Territories, which brings together business leaders, educators, parents, and the community to inspire and educate youth and help them prepare for their future.

Growth, innovation, and creativity—this is how the organization continues its legacy.

Edmonton

Real Estate, Construction, and Development Services

Profiles of Companies and Organizations

Carma Developers

Since 1958, this Alberta land developer has designed ideal communities featuring fine homes for every family and budget, innovative architectural and land development themes, and residents' associations to maintain amenities.

Right: Inverness Square is the central park featured in Inverness Village in McKenzie Towne, Carma Developers' world-renowned neo-traditional community in Calgary, Alberta.

For almost 50 years Carma Developers has enticed new homebuyers with artfully planned communities. Some of Calgary's finest builders partner with Carma to ensure that its neighbourhoods have architectural unity and use the best building materials. Master planning is the company's fundamental design principle, which incorporates the land's special features and geography to create landscaping, parks, and natural reserves that provide residents with beauty, recreation, and a highly satisfying lifestyle.

Carma believes that community means more than houses, streets, and sidewalks. Community is where neighbours share interests, concerns, and the pride of ownership. Carma knits this concept of community into the very fabric of its developments. For example, every new Carma neighbourhood has Carma-Connect, an intranet that residents use to get to know one another. Carma-Connect features message boards, classified ads, e-mail, and more. And Carma develops communities in harmony with the land, letting nature embroider its neighbourhoods. The result: communities that mature gracefully over time.

Inclusive through and through, Carma's communities appeal to people across socioeconomic strata, and thus the company controls a commanding share of the housing markets in Calgary and Edmonton.

The company's in-house builders, Heartland Homes and Hawthorne Homes, share Carma's high standards. Heartland has built quality, affordable homes since 1989. Service and quality have won Heartland the Alberta New Home Warranty Customer Choice Award 10 times since 1992, a streak unmatched by any Calgary builder.

Hawthorne began building multifamily homes in 1995 and works with Carma's land division to plan sites and projects. Its affordable town homes and apartments display the customary high standards. Hawthorne Homes has received the Alberta New Home Warranty Customer

Choice Award four times and also became the CRHBA (Calgary Region Home Builders Association) Multifamily Builder of the Year in 2000.

Carma communities in Calgary include neo-traditional McKenzie Towne, offering the look and feel of small town living right in the city; New Brighton (Carma's first wired community), with a recreational centre, central park, and pond; Cranston, overlooking the Bow River Valley, a landscape that puts city life at the doorstep of nature; Auburn Bay,

a freshwater lake community set in a "cottage country" atmosphere; Tuscany, with the 16,000-square-foot Tuscany Club and a variety of houses so that people can move up within the community; Aspen Hills, located on Calgary's popular westside; The Cascades, located at the top of the city, featuring Arts and Crafts architecture; and 300-acre Seton, a mixed-use development with shops, employment centres, a hospital and health campus, and plans for a high school, park, and million-square-foot shopping centre.

In Edmonton, a freshwater lake and beach accent the Cape Cod motif in Summerside; neotraditional Terwillegar Towne, designed around a town square, evokes the tradition of simpler times; 480-acre Parkland incorporates woods and wetlands for bird-watching and enjoying nature; and Gateway Business Park contains 325 acres of land suitable for suburban office space, warehouses, and other buildings.

Carma strives to always stay on top of new community and housing trends, steadied by judicious business sense, conservative financing,

prescient planning, and top-notch engineering and marketing. Their communities preserve natural beauty, connect residents, and accommodate people's growing and changing needs.

Carma will build more new communities in Edmonton and Calgary and continue investing in its markets outside of Alberta: Austin, Texas; Denver, Colorado; and Kansas City, Missouri. Supported by parent company Brookfield Properties, Carma designs and builds the neighbourhoods where residents can build lasting, close-knit communities.

Above right: Inspired by the simple pleasures of resort living, Carma Developers' Lake Summerside community in Edmonton features beautiful lakefront homes that feature the character and grace of Cape Cod architecture. Above left: Carma's Tuscany was designed to take advantage of the rolling hills, the mountain views, and the 170-acre natural ravine that winds through this northwest Calgary community.

Horton CBI, Limited

This company is a leading designer and builder of hydrocarbon processing systems and storage facilities—including hydrogen plants, sulfur-recovery complexes, storage tanks, terminals, and pressure vessels—for oil, gas, chemical, and petrochemical enterprises throughout Alberta and across Canada.

Right: Horton CBI, Limited crews construct a 110-foot-tall vacuum tower at an oil sands site located near Fort McMurray, Alberta.

Horton CBI, Limited, the Canadian subsidiary of CB&I, has been instrumental in the growth of the oil and gas industry in Canada since the early part of the 20th century. Established in 1916 in Ontario, the company was originally known as Horton Steel Works. The company name was changed to Horton CBI, Limited in 1973. During its more than 90 years of operation in Canada, Horton CBI has become a leader in the design and construction of projects that serve the oil, gas, chemical, and petrochemical industries in every region of the country.

While it has five offices and various project sites strategically located throughout Canada, Horton CBI's headquarters are located near Fort Saskatchewan, Alberta, where the company has an administrative office and equipment warehouse situated on 135 acres of land. Other facilities in Alberta include the company's main sales and marketing office in Calgary and a satellite office in Fort McMurray.

History

Parent company Chicago Bridge & Iron Company N.V., known today as CB&I (with headquarters in the Netherlands and operations around the globe), was established in Chicago, Illinois, in 1889 by Horace Ebenezer Horton. Building upon a heritage of technical innovation, self-reliance, and global resources, CB&I has become one of the world's leading engineering, procurement, and construction (EPC) companies—specializing in projects for clients that produce, process, store, and distribute natural resources.

In late 2000, CB&I initiated a series of acquisitions that expanded its capability to encompass the entire hydrocarbon value chain, from wellhead through processing and distribution. Today's CB&I is a fully integrated, full-service EPC company that can manage the entire scope of large-scale process plant projects, as well as turnkey storage facility projects, virtually anywhere in the world.

Capabilities

As part of the worldwide CB&I organization, Horton CBI has access to the resources, experience, and technologies of a global enterprise. As a local company, Horton CBI is focused on the specific needs of its Albertan customers. Throughout the province, Horton CBI is known for its ability to provide storage tanks and pressure vessels for petrochemical plants, refineries, upgraders, and pipeline facilities. With the added capabilities attained through CB&I's acquisitions in the new millennium, Horton CBI can now also provide hydrogen plants, off-gas processing, and sulfur-recovery complexes to refineries across Alberta.

Safety is a key component of the culture of the entire CB&I organization. Over the years, Horton CBI has achieved a record of exemplary safety performance, which translates directly to lower cost, timely completion of projects, and reduced risk to employees, subcontractors, and customers.

Experience

Horton CBI has been involved in major oil and gas projects executed in Alberta since the 1960s. When oil sands operations (to extract oil from mixtures of sand, water, clay, and bitumen) were started in the 1960s, Horton CBI was on hand to provide the storage facilities needed.

Because maximizing economies of scale is vital to success in the oil sands industry, Horton CBI became a specialty contractor for this market, expanding its ability to design, fabricate, and install large, heavy steel-plate structures— some of which exceed 100 feet in height or diameter. In 1999, Horton CBI designed and built the world's largest vacuum distillation tower, and in 2004 it completed vessels for one of the world's largest fluid coker units.

Building Alberta's and Canada's Future

Horton CBI initiated a major Canadian project in August 2005 when the company was awarded a lump-sum turnkey contract for the design and construction of cryogenic storage tanks for a new liquefied natural gas (LNG) import terminal near Port Hawkesbury in Nova Scotia. The facility, which will be owned and operated by Bear Head LNG Corporation, is designed to meet the growing demand for natural gas in markets in eastern Canada and the U.S. Northeast.

In Alberta, Horton CBI is poised to make major contributions in the design and construction of plant infrastructures for the many upcoming oil sands projects. The company provides additional information on its Web site, www.CBI.com.

With more than 100 employees on permanent staff and construction crews that can peak at more than 600 people, and with a solid history of community involvement and support for local charity organizations, Horton CBI, Limited is proud to participate in the continued growth of Alberta's economy.

Above: Horton CBI constructed these 150,000-barrel-capacity oil sands tanks near Fort McMurray, Alberta.

Homes by Avi Inc.

Homes by Avi has built dream homes for more than 5,000 families in communities throughout Calgary and Edmonton by combining the best in new home design and materials with outstanding attention to detail and personalized service.

In 1978, when residential construction was dominated by big companies and high volume development, Avi Amir and his wife, Rachel, chose to take a different approach by building homes with a superior finish inside and out, paying attention to every detail, and providing personalized service to each family. From the very beginning, Homes by Avi Inc.'s simple yet ambitious vision statement gave the company its direction:

"To be the builder of choice in our markets and to build the dream homes of our customers without causing them any stress." Today the company's 150 employees, at its Calgary headquarters and Edmonton office, work with hundreds of subcontractors and suppliers to fulfill that vision.

Whether the project at hand is a semi-detached duplex or an estate home, Avi sees to it that high standards for quality are met during every phase of construction. Because of this commitment, Homes by Avi offers buyers at every level of the market better choices. From flooring and lighting fixtures to bathtubs and carpet, clients are given a wide range of choices at the 5,000-square-foot selection centre, Avi Definitions, where buyers may customize their homes to suit their individual needs and style preferences.

"We Deliver What We Promise" represents a five-part devotion to quality and service that has always set the company apart from the competition, resulting in repeat business, numerous awards from regional and national home builders associations, and a reputation for mastering the details of new home construction.

- **Guaranteed Trade-In Program:** Homes by Avi guarantees sellers fair market value for existing homes.
- **Six Stage Quality Control Program:** Ensures written documentation of inspections for every new home's cribbing, framing, drywall, finishing, painting, and final inspection.
- **Construction Management:** Promises that every superintendent, manager, and supervisor is a certified moisture control technician.
- **Simplified Customer Service:** One phone number for all inquiries makes the purchase, construction, and ownership of a new home stress-free due to easy access to representatives.
- **Avi Two- and Five-Year Warranty:** Covers all of a home's systems through the second year in addition to the Alberta New Home Warranty, which covers the home's structure and envelope for a full five years.

Due to its core values of fiscal responsibility, honesty, professionalism, reliability, and friendliness, the company has never lost its direction and focus. Homes by Avi, one of Alberta's leading home builders for more than a quarter of a century, designs and builds homes that are safe, durable, comfortable, and beautiful and that really do make dreams come true.

Sinclair Supply Ltd.

A premier wholesale distributor, manufacturer, and custom-fabricator for the HVACR industry throughout western Canada, this company provides quality products and good customer service with thorough knowledge, availability, and competitive pricing.

Sinclair Supply Ltd. (SSL) is an Edmonton, Alberta–based, independent wholesale distributor of residential, commercial, and industrial heating, ventilation, air-conditioning, and refrigeration (HVACR) equipment and controls.

The year 2006 marks a special occasion for the company—SSL celebrates its 60th anniversary. The company is proud to have served the HVACR industry in western Canada and to have shared in the growth and development and the legacy of Alberta's first 100 years.

Founded in 1946 by Walter Sinclair, SSL has grown from its humble beginnings in a two-car garage to 10 branches across western Canada with thousands of square feet of showroom and warehouse space and more than 160 employees.

In the early 1950s, the company was known as Sinclair Stove & Heating—The Plumbers and Tinsmiths Specialty House. Some of its main products then

were woodstoves, gravity-type coal-fired furnaces, chimneys, controls, and an innovative side-armed water heater that it manufactured.

There are presently two SSL locations in Edmonton—the head office and a southside branch. Other locations include Calgary, Lethbridge, Red Deer, and Fort McMurray, Alberta; Regina and Saskatoon, Saskatchewan; and Surrey and Victoria, British Columbia.

SSL distributes more than 400 quality product lines that include more than

30,000 stock items from its industries' most recognized manufacturers. Living up to its name "The Controls Specialists," SSL carries western Canada's largest selection of HVACR controls. A diverse product line of service essentials and a knowledgeable sales staff are on hand to ensure that customers receive the right product for their job application.

Owner and president Dan Sorochan says, "We base our business on providing good customer service, with quality products, thorough

knowledge, product availability, and competitive pricing."

SSL holds memberships in all the major HVACR industry associations and contributes to many charities and community support programs. It contributes to the future educational development of the industries it serves by sponsoring scholarships at the Northern Alberta Institute of Technology (NAIT), the Southern Alberta Institute of Technology (SAIT), and Keyano College.

Sinclair Supply Ltd. is proud of its past 60 years serving the HVACR industry in western Canada and looks forward to the future and to continuing growth in Alberta's vibrant economy.

Above left: Each of Sinclair Supply Ltd.'s 10 branches across western Canada encompasses thousands of square feet of warehouse and showroom space.
Above right: This leading company's head office is located in Edmonton, Alberta.

Cardel Homes

This internationally successful, Calgary-based company began by building one single-family home, and that first project became the basis for a business that today not only builds homes but also helps create communities.

They started small: a husband and wife, both teachers, building a home for their family. As it turned out, people really liked that first home, and before long the family was busy building more homes. Today, the company that Caryl and Del Ockey started in 1973 has grown to international prominence, with operations in Tampa, Florida; Denver, Colorado; Ottawa, Ontario; and Calgary, Alberta.

Over the years Cardel Homes has earned a reputation among trades and developers as a reliable long-term partner. Many of its trades have been with it from the start, secure in the knowledge that their experience and dedication to quality will always have a place at Cardel.

With a product range that includes single-family homes, luxury estate homes, multifamily projects, and resort condominiums, Cardel has built its success on

innovation. Its design department is constantly in motion, drafting new designs for every new community where the company builds. In every region, Cardel's designers strive to create models that invite people inside—at first because of their originality and then by the harmony of form and function that resonates in every room. Increasingly, Cardel is becoming known for projects that are beyond just "great homes." The creation of local landmarks and

amenities such as parks highlight its attention to families' quality of life outside their homes—an area where Cardel believes homebuilders can play a positive role.

Indeed, if people ask anyone at Cardel about the achievement they value most, they will invariably talk about Cardel's Community and Charitable Programs committee and its lasting impact on communities. The objective is to help build great cities—places where people have opportunities to become involved in their communities. In Calgary, Cardel focuses on programs for less-fortunate families, including providing opportunities for children of all backgrounds to go to camp, become involved in sports, and even spend time with local sports stars in special workshops.

A lot has changed since 1973, but in each of its homes and communities, this homebuilder remains true to the spirit and commitment that went into its first home. After 30 years, Cardel is still building homes it is proud to call its own.

Retail

Profiles of Companies and Organizations

Canada Safeway Limited

For more than 75 years, this grocery store icon—one of the largest food retailers in North America—has continually developed innovative ways to serve shoppers by focusing on high quality products, customer service, and community satisfaction.

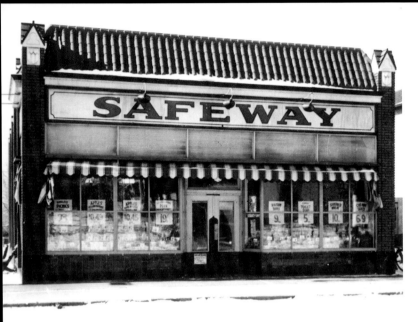

Above: Proudly established in Canada in 1929, Canada Safeway Limited has led the industry in retail innovations and customer service. Then as now, this leading food retailer and its valued employees make a positive impact on the communities in which it operates.

In 1929, when Walter J. Kraft began operating five stores in Canada, grocery stores were not the huge, diversified markets of today. In a typical grocery store of the early 1930s, which covered about 1,000 square feet, customers bought only one or two day's worth of food at a time, because blocks of ice were the standard source of refrigeration. But this would soon change. Widespread electricity brought with it the convenience of home refrigerators and freezers, enabling shoppers to stock up. The ubiquity of the automobile was also pivotal, as it allowed for the transport of larger loads. Another modern idea—selling meat, dairy, grocery and bakery items all under one roof—also revolutionized the industry, causing the average size of grocery stores to grow significantly.

A few of Safeway's innovations designed to complement this new era in grocery shopping were free parking spaces and shopping carts. To accommodate the new shopping method of self-service, Safeway provided weigh scales to help customers buy produce by the pound. Other firsts established by the company included merchandising events, the support of farm and livestock producers, and a guaranteed meat-trim program. By 1936 Piggly Wiggly food stores and A. MacDonald, a food wholesaler, were a part of Canada Safeway's operations. These acquisitions were made to ensure a reliable source of products for the company's growing number of retail stores.

The 1940s and 1950s brought different, yet equally important, forms of growth and achievement. Safeway introduced an employee retirement program for its staff, established employee training and development, and set up the Comic Corral, a place where children could be kept busy while their parents shopped. Another first was open-top, refrigerated display cases, which made products more accessible to shoppers. The 1950s were a time of fierce competition among grocery retailers, whose stores continued to expand in size and scope. In 1952 Safeway introduced its trademark red "S"—for a product line with a money-back satisfaction guarantee. The line eventually became one of the most recognized brands in North America.

By the 1960s Safeway stores were air-conditioned and featured the most advanced freezer cases. In 1966 the company acquired Edmonton-based Jasper Dairy Company, which supplied the stores with a complete line of milk and dairy products. Grand openings of new stores were celebrated by the entire community with music, dancing, and much fanfare. Grocery stores continued to expand, bringing additional benefits for customers, such as lower prices associated with bulk buying and increased self-service.

In the 1980s and 1990s, the average size of a grocery store reached 50,000 square feet. The retail concept of "stores within stores" became popular and called for each department to offer even higher levels of service and product expertise. Safeway was a pioneer in providing in-store pharmacies and floral departments in 1980. It bought the U.S. supermarket chains Vons, Dominick's Finer Foods, and Randall's Food Markets in the 1990s; and started the Club Card, a form of coupon-free discounts, in 1998. In that same year, the Bank of Montreal began opening in-store branches.

The Next Generation

Today, Canada Safeway is focused on providing world-class service to every customer by exceeding their expectations. The development of Safeway's

"Lifestyle" stores is a critical strategy that is designed to continue to set Safeway stores apart. Lifestyle stores are designed for busy customers who want to find everything in one place—great selection, knowledgeable staff, specialty items, and ready-to-eat meals. The Lifestyle stores, some new and some remodeled, feature inviting décor and subdued lighting that create a relaxing atmosphere for shopping.

The many specialized departments of Lifestyle stores include:

- Meat—Experienced employees can offer suggestions for entrées, cut meat according to the shopper's request, and add marinades or seasonings at no extra charge; there are prepared foods, such as stuffed pork loin and other prepared meats and stuffed Cornish game hens.
- Seafood—A self-serve counter enables quick shopping and also provides special services for customers; employees can add marinades, liquid seasonings, or dry rubs to a customer's purchase.

- Produce—This department provides hundreds of fresh items delivered daily. The "Guaranteed Sweet" program is designed to ensure that customers receive the freshest and sweetest products each and every day. Safeway also has expanded its organic produce offerings to include over 40 fresh items daily, as well as a variety of cookbooks and complementary housewares.
- Delicatessen and Food Service—Signature items exclusive to Safeway include fresh, custom-made sandwiches, panini, and an extensive variety of soups. Additionally this expanded department offers an olive bar, over 100 specialty cheeses, dozens of fresh salads, and a wide

assortment of luncheon meats. At Your Table items are ready-to-eat, chef-inspired meals.
- Scratch Bakery—Professionals bake fresh bakery goods daily; a wide selection of breads and desserts include made-to-order cakes and European-style artisan desserts made with Belgian chocolate and other imported ingredients, creamery butter, and freshly whipped cream.
- Gifts and Flowers—Shoppers will find an assortment of fresh plants and flowers and may request custom-designed arrangements; in addition, there are home décor and gift items, novelty chocolates, scented candles, vases, pottery, and cards.

Additional conveniences are offered at many Lifestyle stores, such as a full-service Starbucks coffee shop, an in-store seating area, and an in-store Bank of Montreal kiosk. With its commitment to providing greater selection and convenience for today's busy customers, Safeway has defined and exemplified the next generation in shopping.

Because They Care

For more than 75 years Canada Safeway has supported thousands of western Canada's health and family causes. Annually, Safeway and its 28,500 employees provide over $15 million in contributions to organizations that assist families and youth, hospitals and health programs, neighborhood-based causes, and food banks. Together with its thousands of employees and on behalf of its millions of customers, this conscientious company has made a lasting impact on the community.

Above left: In order to better serve its customers, Canada Safeway offers comprehensive training and development programs to help employees become experts in their particular fields. Above right: Canada Safeway operates 214 stores, which are located primarily in Alberta, British Columbia, Manitoba, Saskatchewan, and northwestern Ontario.

Cherbo Publishing Group

Cherbo Publishing Group's business-focused, art book–quality publications, which celebrate the vital spirit of enterprise, are custom books that are used as high-impact economic development tools to enhance reputations, increase profits, and provide global exposure for businesses and organizations.

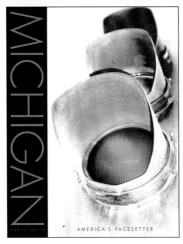

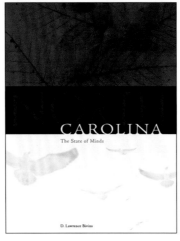

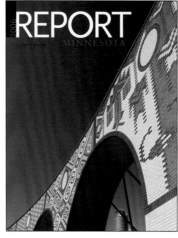

The Story Behind Cherbo Publishing Group (CPG)

Jack Cherbo, Cherbo Publishing Group president and CEO, has been breaking new ground in the sponsored publishing business for more than 40 years.

"Previously, the cost of creating a handsome book for business developments or commemorative occasions fell directly on the sponsoring organization," Cherbo says. "My company pioneered an entirely new concept—funding these books through the sale of corporate profiles."

Cherbo honed his leading edge in Chicago, where he owned a top advertising agency before moving into publishing. Armed with a degree in business administration from Northwestern University, a mind that never stopped, and a keen sense of humor, Cherbo set out to succeed—and continues to do just that.

CPG is North America's leading publisher of quality custom books for commercial, civic, historical, and trade associations. Publications range from hardcover state, regional, and commemorative books to softcover state and regional business reports. Formerly a wholly owned subsidiary of Jostens, Inc., a Fortune 500 company, CPG has been a privately held corporation since 1993. The company is headquartered in Encino, California, and operates regional offices in Philadelphia, Minneapolis, and Houston.

Who Uses CPG's Services?

CPG has created books for some of America's leading organizations, including the U.S. Chamber of Commerce, Empire State Development, California Sesquicentennial Foundation, Chicago O'Hare International Airport, and the Indiana Manufacturers Association. Participants have included ConAgra, Dow Chemical Company, Lucent Technologies, Merck & Company, and BlueCross/BlueShield.

About CPG Publications

CPG series range from history books to economic development/relocation books and from business reports to publications of special interest.

The economic development series spotlights fast-growing cities, regions, or states, showcasing the outstanding economic and quality-of-life advantages. The annual business reports provide an economic snapshot of individual cities, regions, or states. The commemorative series marks milestones for corporations, organizations, and professional and trade associations.

To find out how CPG can help you celebrate a special occasion, or for information on how to showcase your company or organization, contact Jack Cherbo at 818-783-0040, extension 26, or visit www.cherbopub.com.

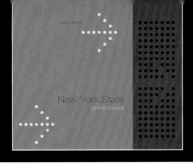
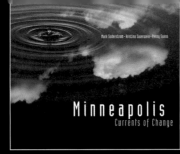

Select CPG Publications

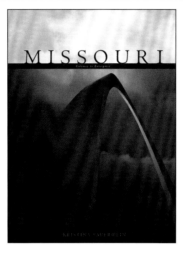
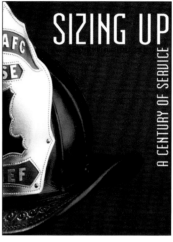
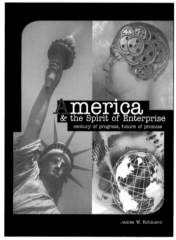

VISIONS OF OPPORTUNITY
City, Regional, and State Series

AMERICA & THE SPIRIT OF ENTERPRISE
Century of Progress, Future of Promise

CALIFORNIA *Golden Past, Shining Future*

CONNECTICUT *Chartered for Progress*

DELAWARE
Incorporating Vision in Industry

DUPAGE COUNTY, ILLINOIS
Economic Powerhouse

EVANSVILLE
At the Heart of Success

GREATER PHOENIX
Expanding Horizons

MICHIGAN *America's Pacesetter*

MILWAUKEE *Midwestern Metropolis*

MISSOURI *Gateway to Enterprise*

NEW YORK STATE *Prime Mover*

NORTH CAROLINA *The State of Minds*

SOUTH DAKOTA
Pioneering the Future

UPSTATE NEW YORK
Corridor to Progress

WESTCHESTER COUNTY, NEW YORK
Headquarters to the World

WEST VIRGINIA
Reaching New Heights

LEGACY
Commemorative Series

BUILD IT & THE CROWDS WILL COME
Seventy-Five Years of Public Assembly

CELEBRATE SAINT PAUL
150 Years of History

DAYTON
On the Wings of Progress

THE EXHIBITION INDUSTRY
The Power of Commerce

MINNEAPOLIS
Currents of Change

NEW YORK STATE ASSOCIATION OF FIRE CHIEFS
Sizing Up a Century of Service

VISIONS TAKING SHAPE
Celebrating 50 Years of the Precast/ Prestressed Concrete Industry

ANNUAL BUSINESS REPORTS

MINNESOTA REPORT *2006*

BIBLIOGRAPHY

Acland, Joan. "Cardinal, Douglas Joseph." *The Canadian Encyclopedia*. <http://66.59.133.172/index.cfm?PgNm=TCE&Params=A1ARTA0001394> (2005).

"Agriculture and Calgary's First Skyscraper." *Edmonton Journal*, May 27, 2005. <http://www.canada.com/edmonton/edmontonjournal/features/100days/story.html?id=79c60bf9-03d2-4b3d2-4b3d-a4e9-45b59e536d44> (2005).

"Agri-Cures." *Edmonton Journal*, May 27, 2005. <http://www.canada.com/edmonton/edmontonjournal/features/100days/story.html?id=5211a70c-5372-4435-97c0-d4206399309f> (2005).

Alberta Department of Agriculture. *A Historical Series of Agricultural Statistics for Alberta*. Edmonton: Alberta Department of Agriculture, 1966.

———. *Alberta Agriculture: A History in Graphs*. Edmonton: Alberta Department of Agriculture, 1972.

"Alberta Economic Presence Profile 2004." Canadian Pacific Railway (fact sheet), 2005.

"Alberta: Economy." Education Canada. <http://educationcanada.com/facts/index.phtml?sid=ab&a=4&lang=eng> (2005).

Alberta Family Histories Society. "Alberta Timeline." <http://www.afhs.ab.ca/data/timeline.html> (2005).

Alberta Historic Sites Service. *Coal Mining in Crowsnest Pass*. Edmonton: Alberta Culture, 1985.

"Alberta: History and People." Education Canada. <http://educationcanada.com/facts/index.phtml?sid=ab&a=3&lang=eng> (2005).

Alberta Legislature. "Building Tour Outline." <http://www.assembly.ab.ca/visitor/facts/index.htm> (2005).

Alberta Roadbuilders and Heavy Construction Association. *Shaping Alberta: A History of the Alberta Roadbuilders and Heavy Construction Association*. Edmonton: Alberta Roadbuilders and Heavy Construction Association, 1991.

"Alberta's Thriving Forest Industry." Alberta Economic Development. <http://alberta-canada.com/forest/index.cfm> (2005).

"Alberta Tourism Quick Facts." Alberta Economic Development (brochure), June 2005. <http://www.alberta-canada.com/statpub/economicHighlights/factsOnAlberta.cfm> (2005).

Allan, John A. *Coal Areas of Alberta*. Edmonton: Research Council of Alberta, 1943.

Amrhein, Dr. Carl. "'Campus Alberta' Has Big Role in Province's 20-Year Economic Plan." University of Alberta (press release), August 12, 2005. <http://www.express-news.ualberta.ca/article.cfm?id=6872> (2005).

Annual Report 2004–2005. Alberta Transportation and Infrastructure. <http://www.inftra.gov.ab.ca/> (2005).

Annual Reports 1905–1972. Alberta Department of Public Works.

Anton, Frank R. *The Canadian Coal Industry: Challenge in the Years Ahead*. Calgary: Detselig Enterprises, 1981.

The Applied History Research Group, University of Calgary. "Calgary and Southern Alberta: Disastrous Consequences." <http://www.ucalgary.ca/applied_history/tutor/calgary/disaster.html> (2005).

———. "Calgary and Southern Alberta: Fort Calgary, 1875–1894." <http://www.ucalgary.ca/applied_history/tutor/calgary/FRAME1875.html> (2005).

———. "Calgary and Southern Alberta: The North-West Mounted Police." <http://www.ucalgary.ca/applied_history/tutor/calgary/FRAME1875.html> (2005).

———. "Calgary and Southern Alberta: Solutions to the Problems of Dryland Farming." <http://ucalgary.ca/applied_history/tutor/calgary/dryland.html> (2005).

———. "Post-Leduc Oil and Gas Exploration and Development." <http://www.ucalgary.ca/applied_history/tutor/calgary/FRAMEoil.html> (2005).

———. "Ranching." <http://www.ucalgary.ca/applied_history/tutor/calgary/ranch.html> (2005).

———. "Social and Cultural Developments." <http://www.ucalgary.ca/applied_history/tutor/frontiersoc.html> (2005).

———. "The Turner Valley Oil Era: 1913–1946." <http://www.ucalgary.ca/applied_history/tutor/calgary/FRAMEoil.html> (2005).

ATB Financial. *Albertans Investing in Alberta*. ATB Financial. <http:www.atb.com/dev/aboutatb/atb_book.asp> (2005).

Baines, Audrey S. *From Cottage to Composite, 1886–1986: Lethbridge School District No. 51, The First 100 Years*. Lethbridge: Lethbridge School District No. 51, 1985.

Bercuson, David Jay, ed. *Alberta's Coal Industry, 1919*. Calgary: Alberta Records Publication Board, Historical Society of Alberta, 1978.

Berton, Pierre. *The Last Spike: The Great Railway, 1881–1885*. Toronto: McClelland and Stewart, 1971.

Board, Mike. "Tourist Gold Legacy of Winter Olympics." *Calgary Herald*, February 12, 1989.

Boddy, Trevor. *Modern Architecture in Alberta*. Regina: Alberta Culture and Multiculturalism and the Plains Research Centre, 1987.

———. *The Architecture of Douglas Cardinal*. Edmonton: NeWest Press, 1989.

Bone, P. Turner. *When the Steel Went Through: Reminiscences of a Railway Pioneer*. Toronto: Macmillan, 1947.

Brado, Edward. *Cattle Kingdom: Early Ranching in Alberta*. Vancouver: Douglas & McIntyre, 1984.

Breen, David H. *The Canadian Prairie West and the Ranching Frontier, 1874–1924*. Toronto: University of Toronto Press, 1983.

Buziak, Kelly Jane. *Toiling in the Woods: Aspects of the Lumber Business in Alberta to 1930*. Wetaskiwin: Friends of Reynolds-Alberta Museum Society and Alberta Culture and Multiculturalism, Historic Sites and Archives Service, 1992.

"Canadian Pacific Railway Brings IBM on Board to Manage Computing Infrastructure." Canadian Pacific Railway (press release), December 2, 2003. <http:www.newswire.ca.en/releases/archive/December2003/02/c8390.html> (2005).

Cashman, Anthony Walcott. *A History of Motoring in Alberta*. Edmonton: Alberta Motor Association, 1990.

———. *The Alberta Motor Association: A History*. Edmonton: Alberta Motor Association, 1967.

Cass, Douglas E. "Investment in the Alberta Petroleum Industry, 1912–1930." Master's thesis. University of Calgary, 1985.

"Celebrate Ranches." The Applied History Research Group, University of Calgary. <http://www.ucalgary.ca/applied_history/tutor/calgary/celebranches.html> (2005).

Chalmers, John W. *Schools of the Foothills Province*. Toronto: University of Toronto Press, 1967.

Chastko, Paul. *Developing Alberta's Oil Sands: From Karl Clark to Kyoto*. Calgary: University of Calgary Press, 2004.

Coates, Kenneth. *North to Alaska*. Toronto: McClelland & Stewart, 1992.

Corbet, Elise A. *Frontiers of Medicine: A History of Medical Education and Research at the University of Alberta*. Edmonton: University of Alberta Press, 1990.

Cruickshank, Scott. "Calgary to Host '06 Worlds." *Calgary Herald*, June 5, 2003, sec. F.

Davis, Anthony, Dina O'Meara and Gordon Cope. "Health Care 2004." *Alberta Venture*, 8 (December 2004): 75–92.

Dawe, Harold. *Schools at the Crossing: A History of the Red Deer Public School District No. 104*. Red Deer: Red Deer Public School District, 1992.

De Mille, George. *Oil in Canada West, The Early Years*. Calgary: Northwest Print and Lithographing, 1970.

den Otter, Andrew A. *Sir Alexander T. Galt and the Northwest: A Case Study of Entrepreneurialism on the Frontier*. Edmonton: University of Alberta, 1975.

———. "A Social History of the Alberta Coal Branch." Master's thesis. University of Alberta, 1967.

BIBLIOGRAPHY

Department of History, University of Calgary. "The CPR and the Development of Calgary."<http://www.alf.sd83.bc.ca/ALFWeb3.0/departments/humanities/SS101/Reg_Geog_History/praries/cprcalgary.html> (2005).

Dingwall, Gloria Ann. *100: A Western Portrait*. Calgary: G. Dingwall, 2003.

"Dr. William Fairfield." *Edmonton Journal*, May 26, 2005. <http://www.canada.com.aspx?id=75fd2f88-9ba0-4802-a891-b1d2a5dcf57b> (2005).

Dolphin, Frank, and John Dolphin. *Country Power: The Electrical Revolution in Rural Alberta*. Edmonton: Plains, 1993.

Drummond, W. M., and W. Mackenzie. *Progress and Prospects of Canadian Agriculture*. Ottawa: Royal Commission on Canada's Economic Prospects, 1957.

Eagle, John A. *The Canadian Pacific Railway and the Development of Western Canada, 1896–1914*. Kingston: McGill-Queen's University Press, 1989.

"Electricity—The Magic Medium." IEEE Canada. <http://ieee.ca.diglib/library/electricity/pdf/P_one_7.pdf> (2005).

Evans, Simon M. *The Bar U and Canadian Ranching History*. Calgary: University of Calgary Press, 2004.

———. "The Passing of a Frontier: Ranching In the Canadian West, 1882–1912." Ph.D. thesis. University of Calgary, 1976.

"Facts About the Alberta Agri-Food Industry." Alberta Economic Development. <http://alberta-canada.com/agric/indFacts.cfm> (2005).

"Father Albert Lacombe." *Edmonton Journal*, May 27, 2005. <http:www.canada.com/edmonton/edmontonjournal/features/100days/story.htmlid=b67c305b-fbb3-4cd5-bf86-d6740f042906> (2005).

Ferguson, Barry. *Athabasca Oil Sands*. Edmonton: Alberta Culture, 1985.

XV Olympic Winter Games, Official Report. XV Olympic Winter Games Organizing Committee, Calgary Olympic Development Association, 1987.

Finch, David. *Albertans Investing in Alberta*. Edmonton: Alberta Treasury Branches, 1999.

———. *Much Brain and Sinew*. Brooks: Eastern Irrigation District, 1993.

———. "Turner Valley Oilfield Development, 1914–1945." Master's thesis. University of Calgary, 1985.

———, and Gordon Jaremko. *Fields of Fire: An Illustrated History of Canadian Petroleum*. Calgary: Detselig Enterprises, 1994.

Foran, Maxwell. *Calgary: An Illustrated History*. Toronto: J. Lorimer and National Museum of Man, National Museums of Canada, 1978.

———. *Trails and Trials: Markets and Land Use in the Alberta Beef Cattle Industry, 1881–1948*. Calgary: University of Calgary Press, 2003.

———, and Heather MacEwan Foran. *Calgary: Canada's Frontier Metropolis: An Illustrated History*. Burlington: Windsor, 1982.

Fraser, Linda. "Rule Wynn and Rule." *The Canadian Encyclopedia*. <http://thecanadianencyclopedia.com/index.cfm?PgNm=TCE&Params=A1ARTA0009551> (2005).

Gilpin, John. *Edmonton: Gateway to the North*. Woodland Hills: Windsor Publications, 1984.

Gould, Ed. *Ranching: Ranching in Western Canada*. Saanichton: Hancock House, 1978.

Government of Alberta. "Enjoying Alberta: Father Lacombe Chapel." <http://www.cd.gov.ab.ca/enjoying_alberta/museums_historic_sites/site_listings/father_lacombe/index.asp> (2005).

———. "Enjoying Alberta: Frank Slide." <http://www.cd.gov.ab.ca/enjoying_alberta/museums_historic_sites/site_listings/frank_slide/index.asp> (2005).

———. "Enjoying Alberta: Turner Valley Gas Plant." <http://www.cd.gov.ab.ca/enjoying_alberta/museums_historic_sites/site_listings/turner_valley/index.asp> (2005).

———. "Fur Trade." <http://www.gov.ab.ca/home/index.cfm?Page=28> (2005).

———. "Preserving Alberta: Provincial Archives of Alberta." <http://www.cd.gov.ab.ca/preserving/index.asp> (2005).

———. "Who Was John Ware?" <http://www.albertacentennial.ca/history/
viewpost.aspx?id=245> (2005).

Granson, Ernest, Will Gibson and Dan Rubenstein. "Industry Report Forestry
2005." *Alberta Venture*, 9 (March 2005): 109-131.

Gray, James Henry. *A Brand of Its Own: The 100 Year History of the Calgary
Exhibition and Stampede.* Saskatoon: Western Producer Prairie Books, 1985.

———. *R. B. Bennett: The Calgary Years.* Toronto: University of Toronto
Press, 1991.

Gregory, Joe. "Minding the Land." *Edmonton Journal*, March 14, 2005.
<http://www.canada.com/calgary/calgaryherald/features/agreport2005/story.html?id=
6e1f2bdd-d5cf-4e50-b94a-4133119ee0bc> (2005).

Guimond, Pierre, and Brian Sinclair. *Calgary Architecture: The Boom Years, 1972–1982.*
Calgary: Detselig Enterprises, 1984.

"Guy Weadick's Festival Vision." *Edmonton Journal*, May 27, 2005.
<http://www.canada.com/edmonton/edmontonjournal/features/100days/
story.html?id=8434df2b-61e0-44ed-9fea-d081de42ar53> (2005).

Hall, David J. "North-West Territories Act." *The Canadian Encyclopedia.*
<http://tceplus.com/index.cfm?PgNm=TCE&Params=A1ARTA0005804> (2005).

Hart, Edward J. *Exploring the Heritage of the Banff-Bow Valley.* Banff: EJH Literary
Enterprises, 1999.

———. *The Selling of Canada: The CPR and the Beginnings of Canadian Tourism.*
Banff: Altitude Publishing, 1983.

Hawkins, W. E. *Electrifying Calgary—A Century of Public and Private Power.*
Calgary: University of Calgary Press, 1987.

Hedges, James. *Building the Canadian West: The Land and Colonization Policies
of the Canadian Pacific Railway.* New York: Macmillan, 1939.

Heritage Community Foundation. "Alberta Rural Life: Early Rural Life."
<http://collections.ic.gc.ca/pasttopresent/rural_life/index.html> (2005).

———. "Alberta Rural Life: Ranching in the Years 1914–1920."
<http://www.abheritage.ca/pasttopresent/rural_life/abhistory_ranching.html>
(2005).

———. "Competitive Fur Trade (1850–1900)." <http://www.abheritage.ca/
alberta/fur_trade/overview_pg6_compete.html> (2005).

———. "European Fur Traders Reach Alberta (1778–1795)."
<http://www.abheritage.ca/alberta/fur_trade/overview_pg3_reachAb.html> (2005).

———. "Exploration and Map Making." <http://www.abheritage.ca/alberta/
fur_trade/map_making.html> (2005).

———. "The Hudson's Bay Company's Monopoly (1821–1850)."
<http://www.abheritage.ca/alberta/fur_trade/overview_pg5_hudsons.html> (2005).

———. "John McDougall." <http://www.abheritage.ca/alberta/fur_trade/bio_john_
mcdougall.html> (2005).

———. "Site Profile: Father Lacombe Chapel, St. Albert." <http://www.abheritage.ca/
alberta/fur_trade/site_profiles_father_lacombe.html> (2005).

———. "Site Profile: Fort Edmonton." <http://www.abheritage.ca/alberta/fur_trade/
site_profiles_fort_edmonton.html> (2005).

———. "Traders, Missionaries, and Explorers." <http://www.abheritage.ca/alberta/
fur_trade/overview_pg2_tradeEx.html> (2005).

———. "When Coal Was King: Historical Overview." <http://www.coalking.ca/
industry/historical_4.html> (2005).

Hesketh, Bob, ed. *Three Northern Wartime Projects.* Edmonton: Circumpolar
Institute, University of Alberta, and Edmonton and District Historical
Society, 1996.

Hilborn, James D. *Dusters and Gushers: The Canadian Oil and Gas Industry. By
Outstanding Authorities in the Petroleum and Related Industries.* Toronto: Pitt, 1968.

"History of Alberta Road Development." Alberta Transportation and Infrastructure
(fact sheet), 2005.

BIBLIOGRAPHY

Hursey, Roberta L. *Trucking North on Canada's Mackenzie Highway.* Calgary: Detselig Enterprises, 2000.

Johns, Walter H. *A History of the University of Alberta, 1908–1969.* Edmonton: University of Alberta Press, 1981.

Jones, Llewellyn May. "The Search for Hydrocarbons: Petroleum and Natural Gas in Western Canada, 1883–1947." Master's thesis. University of Calgary, 1978.

Karsten, Peter. "The Calgary Zoo: Past, Present and Future." *Dinny's Digest,* Winter 1989.

Kerr, Aubrey. *Leduc.* Calgary: S.A. Kerr, 1991.

Klassen, Henry. *A Business History of Alberta.* Calgary: University of Calgary Press, 1999.

Knafla, Louis. *Lords of the Western Bench: A Biographical History of the Supreme and District Courts of Alberta, 1876–1990.* Calgary: Legal Archives Society of Alberta, 1997.

Kostek, M. A. *Looking Back: A Century of Education in Edmonton Public Schools.* Edmonton: Edmonton Public School Board, 1982.

Ladouceur, Mark, ed. *The History of Fording Coal Limited.* Calgary: Fording Coal Limited, 1991.

Lamb, W. Kaye. *History of the Canadian Pacific Railway.* New York: Macmillan, 1977.

Larmour, Judy. *Laying Down the Lines: A History of Land Surveying in Alberta.* Calgary: Brindle and Glass, 2005.

Lee, Helen. *The Forest Industry in Alberta, 1870–1955.* Edmonton: Alberta Culture, 1984.

Losey, Timothy. *History of the Automobile in Alberta, 1900–1955.* Edmonton: Reynolds-Alberta Museum, Alberta Culture, 1984.

Lothian, William Fergus. *A History of Canada's National Parks.* Ottawa: Indian and Northern Affairs, Parks Canada, 1976.

MacEwan, Grant. *Frederick Haultain, Frontier Statesman of the Canadian Northwest.* Saskatoon: Western Producer Prairie Books, 1985.

MacEwan, John Walter Grant. *Pat Burns, Cattle King.* Saskatoon: Western Producer Prairie Books, 1979.

"Mad Cow in Canada: The Science and the Story." CBC News Online, July 15, 2005. <http://www.cbc.ca/news/background/madcow> (2005).

"Major Crop Production, Canada and Provinces, 1995–2004." Agriculture, Food, and Rural Development. <http://www1.agric.gov.ab.ca/$department/deptdocs.nsf/all/sdd4339> (2005).

Marck, Paul. "Stantec Bags 'Big Board' Listing; A First For City." University of Alberta Faculty of Engineering. <http://www.engineering.ualberta.ca/nav02.cfm?nav02=37435&nav01=18430> (2005).

Matheson, Shirlee Smith. *A Western Welcome to the World: Calgary International Airport.* Encino: Cherbo Publishing Group, 1997.

Maydonik, Allen. *The Luscar Story.* Edmonton: Luscar Limited, 1985.

McGrath, Tom M. *History of Canadian Airports.* Toronto: Lugus, 1992.

McKenzie-Brown, Peter, and Gordon Jaremko, and David Finch. *The Great Oil Age.* Calgary: Petroleum History Society, 1993.

Myers, Patricia A. *Sky Riders: An Illustrated History of Aviation in Alberta, 1906–1945.* Saskatoon: Fifth House, 1995.

Perry, Dr. Richard, and Ryan Leskiw. "A Century of Alberta Innovation." *BioZine,* 2005.

Petroleum History Society. *Historic Turner Valley: Cradle of Western Canada's Oil and Gas Industry.* Calgary: Petroleum History Society, 2000.

Regehr, T.D., ed. *The Possibilities of Canada Are Truly Great: Memoirs, 1906–1924.* Toronto: Macmillan, 1971.

Rich, Edwin Ernest. *The Fur Trade and the Northwest to 1857.* Toronto: McClelland and Stewart, 1967.

Robertson, Lloyd, and Brian D. Johnson. *The Official Commemorative Book: XV Olympic Winter Games.* Toronto: Key Porter Books, 1988.

Rubak, Paul M. *Big Wheels across the Prairie: A History of Alberta's Trucking Industry.* Calgary: BWATP, 2003.

Stahl, Len. *A Record of Service: The History of Western Canada's Pioneer Gas and Electric Utilities.* Edmonton: Canadian Utilities Limited, 1987.

Stamp, Robert. *School Days: A Century of Memories.* Calgary: Calgary Board of Education, McClelland and Stewart West, 1975.

"The 'Persons' Case, 1927–1929." Library and Archives Canada. <http://www.collectionscanada.ca/famous5/053002_e.html> (2005).

TransCanada Pipeline Company. *The Builders: A Celebration of Achievement.* Toronto: TransCanada Pipelines, 1989.

University of Alberta. "University of Alberta Facts 2005–2006." <http://www.uofaweb.ualberta.ca/facts/> (2005).

Workers' Compensation Board–Alberta. "Cargill Foods and Nusco Manufacturing and Supply Ltd. Win Top Safety Awards" (press release), February 28, 2002. <http://www.wcb.ab.ca/news/2002/020228.asp> (2005).

The Web sites of the following companies and organizations were also consulted:

About.com, Agriculture, Food, and Rural Development, Alberta College of Art and Design, Alberta Dairy Council, Alberta Economic Development, Alberta Forest Products Association, Alberta Government, Alberta Heritage Foundation for Medical Research, Alberta Ingenuity Fund, Alberta Research Council, Answers.com, ATB Financial, ATCO Electric, ATCO Group, Athabasca University, Augustana University, The Banff Centre, Banff Lake Louise Tourism, Bank of Montreal, BBC News, BCMP Architects, Bennett Jones, Calgary International Airport, Calgary Public Library, Calgary Stampede, Calgary Stampeders, Calgary Zoo, Canada.com, Canadian Centre for Energy Information, Canadian Heritage, Canadian Natural, Canadian Pacific Railway, Canadian Tourism Commission, Canadian University College, Canadian Western Bank, CANAMEX Corridor Project, Canfor, Cargill, CIBC, City of Brooks, City of Red Deer, Cohos Evamy, Department of Justice Canada, Douglas J. Cardinal Architect Ltd., Edmonton Airports, Edmonton Public Library, Ellison Milling Company, EnCana, ENMAX, EPCOR, FindAlberta.com, Focus Corporation, Foothills Creamery, Fording Canadian Coal Trust, Foreign Affairs Canada, Fort Museum of the North West Mounted Police, Frank Slide Interpretive Centre, Glenbow Museum, Government of Alberta, Government of Canada, Grande Prairie Regional College, Growing Alberta, Head-Smashed-In Buffalo Jump, Heritage Community Foundation, Heritage Tourism Corporation, The Historical Museum of Bonnyville, Historical Society of Alberta, Hoover's Online, Husky Energy, Imperial Oil, Industry Canada, Innovation Alberta, Kenn Borek Air, Lakeland College, Lakeside Packers, Lamb Weston, Legislative Assembly of Alberta, Lethbridge Community College, Library and Archives Canada, Luscar Ltd., MacEwan College, McCain Foods Limited, Medicine Hat College, The Michael J. Fox Foundation for Parkinson's Research, Mount Royal College, MSN Encarta, Mullen Group, Municipality of Crowsnest Pass, National Institute for Nanotechnology, National Park Service, National Research Council Canada, Natural Resources Canada, Nilsson Bros., NorQuest College, Odyssium, Olds College, Parks Canada, Parmalat, PCL, Petro-Canada, Protein Engineering Network Centres of Excellence, Red Deer College, Rogers Sugar, Royal Alberta Museum, Royal Bank of Canada, Royal Tyrrell Museum, Saputo, Schroeder Milling, Scotiabank, Separation of Alberta, Shell Canada, Skate Canada, Southern Alberta Institute of Technology, SPG Media, Stantec, Suncor Energy, Sustainable Forest Management Network, Syncrude, TD Bank, TheFreeDictionary.com, Town of Fort Macleod, TransAlta, Travel Alberta, Trimac Group, Triple Five Group, United Nations Education, University of Alberta, University of Calgary, University of Calgary Applied History Research Group, University of Calgary Department of History, University of Lethbridge, Waterton Park Information Services, West Edmonton Mall, West Fraser Timber Company, WestJet, Weyerhaeuser Canada, Wikipedia, XL Foods, Yahoo! Finance

INDEX

INDEX

PHOTO CREDITS

Pages ii, iii: © Jim Wiebe/ Panoramic Images

Page v: © Paul A. Souders/Corbis

Pages vi: © Bill Brooks/Masterfile

Page viii: © Daryl Benson/Getty Images

Page ix: © Darrell Lecorre/ Masterfile

Page x: © Richard Cummins/ Corbis

Page xiii: © John Feingersh/ Masterfile

Page xv: © North Light Images/ age fotostock

Page xvi: Courtesy, Glenbow Archives NA-1406–45

Page xvi: Courtesy, Glenbow Archives NA-19–1

Page xvi: Courtesy, Glenbow Archives NA-789–150

Page xvii: Courtesy, Glenbow Archives NA-266–3

Page xvii: Courtesy, Glenbow Archives NA-2977–49

Page xviii: Courtesy, the City of Edmonton Archives

Page xix: Courtesy, Canada Science and Technology Museum

Page xx: Courtesy, Glenbow Archives NA-2864-13287a–1

Page xx: Courtesy, Glenbow Archives ND-8–190

Page xx: Courtesy, Glenbow Archives NA-5470–3

Page xxi: Courtesy, Glenbow Archives NB-54–527

Page xxi: Courtesy, Glenbow Archives NA-2956–5

Page xxi: Courtesy, Glenbow Archives NA-1524–1

Page xxi: Courtesy, Glenbow Archives PA-3672–4

Page xxi: Courtesy, Glenbow Archives C230–16

Page xxii: © Bruce Bennett Studios/Getty Images

Page xxii: © Corey Hochachka/ Design Pics/age fotostock

Page xxiii: © Gunter Marx Photography/Corbis

Page xxiii: Harry How/Getty Images

Page 3: © Janet Bailey/Masterfile

Page 4: © Gloria H. Chomica/ Masterfile

Page 6: Courtesy, Glenbow Archives NA-1534–1

PHOTO CREDITS

CPG

cherbo publishing group, inc.

Typography

Principal faces used: Adobe Garamond, designed by Robert Slimbach in 1989,
which was derived from previous designs by Claude Garamond, Jean Jannon, and
Robert Granjon; Univers, designed by Adrian Frutiger in 1957; Helvetica, designed
by Matthew Carter, Edouard Hoffmann, and Max Miedinger in 1959; and
Industria, designed by Neville Brody in 1989.

Hardware

Macintosh G5 desktops, digital color laser printing with Xerox Docucolor 12, digital
imaging with Creo EverSmart Supreme

Software

QuarkXPress, Adobe Illustrator, Adobe Photoshop, Adobe Acrobat, Microsoft Word,
Eye-One Pro by Gretagmacbeth, Creo Oxygen, FlightCheck

CTP, Printing, and Binding

Performed by Friesens of Altona, Manitoba, Canada
Minneapolis, Minnesota, USA

Paper

Text Paper: #80 Luna Matte

Bound in Rainbow® recycled content papers from
Ecological Fibers, Inc.

Dust Jacket: #100 Sterling-Litho Gloss

Alberta at 100: Celebrating the Legacy